SON TAY 1970

The Operation Ivory Coast
POW rescue mission

Justin W. Williamson

OSPREY PUBLISHING
Bloomsbury Publishing Plc
Kemp House, Chawley Park, Cumnor Hill, Oxford OX2 9PH, UK
29 Earlsfort Terrace, Dublin 2, Ireland
1385 Broadway, 5th Floor, New York, NY 10018, USA
Email: info@ospreypublishing.com
www.ospreypublishing.com

OSPREY is a trademark of Osprey Publishing Ltd

First published in Great Britain in 2024

A catalog record for this book is available from the British Library.

ISBN: PB 9781472863010 eBook 9781472863027;
ePDF 9781472863041; XML 9781472863034

24 25 26 27 28   10 9 8 7 6 5 4 3 2 1

Battlescenes by Edouard A. Groult
Cover art by Irene Cano Rodríguez
Maps by www.bounford.com
3D BEV by Alan Gilliland
Index by Zoe Ross
Typeset by PDQ Digital Media Solutions, Bungay, UK
Printed by Repro India Ltd.

Osprey Publishing supports the Woodland Trust, the UK's leading
woodland conservation charity.

To find out more about our authors and books visit
www.ospreypublishing.com. Here you will find extracts, author
interviews, details of forthcoming events and the option to sign up for our
newsletter.

Author's Note
The views expressed herein belong solely to the author and do not
necessarily reflect those of the US government.

CONTENTS

INTRODUCTION

Efforts to Find the Prisoners of War

In the 1960s, as the ferocious war in Vietnam continued to escalate, the number of Americans captured and missing increased proportionally. Whether they were aircrews shot down and captured, or soldiers and Marines captured in ambushes, the missing and known prisoners of war weighed heavily on the minds of the American public and military. By 1970, the Joint Personnel Recovery Center (JPRC), established in 1966, reported the number of missing and captured as:

Service	Missing	Captured
USAF	513	217
US Army	291	57
US Navy	118	138
USMC	91	26
Civilians	11	31
Total	1024	469

Knowing Americans faced torture or execution when captured, a large-scale effort to retrieve them operated throughout Southeast Asia. Primary responsibility for finding and rescuing Americans fell on the Military Assistance Command, Vietnam – Studies and Observation Group (MACV-SOG), but if additional forces were required, they could be requested from the Commander in Chief, Pacific Fleet (CINCPAC). MACV-SOG took the assignment to heart, with over four dozen of their own men reported missing and at least 15 likely captured. Highly dangerous Air Force Combat Search and Rescue (CSAR) missions retrieved 980 aircrews between 1966 and 1970 in Laos, South Vietnam, and North Vietnam. The US Navy also scoured the waters and battlefields, rescuing its aircrews. Between 1965 and 1968, Navy efforts rescued 458 aircrews. The CSAR missions came at a high

On July 6, 1966, 52 American POWs were marched two miles through the streets of Hanoi in an attempt by North Vietnam to draw attention to the suffering of the population at the hands of American bombers. Instead, a jeering, angry population tried to get to the obviously mistreated POWs, and confirmed in the international community's mind that POWs were being poorly treated and held under extremely adverse conditions. (USAF)

price and, before the war ended, 71 Air Force personnel were killed and 41 aircraft were destroyed. The Navy lost 26 men during rescue attempts, with 33 aircraft destroyed.

North Vietnam, despite being a 1958 signatory of the Geneva Convention, was not forthcoming with details of what POWs they held, treated them brutally, and cynically exploited them for propaganda. In front of television cameras, POWs read false confessions or said their treatment was fair. To expose this lie, one POW, Commander Jeremiah Denton, blinked out the word "Torture" in Morse code. Messages passed to American anti-war activists visiting Hanoi described their harsh treatment. POWs released by the North confirmed their experience of brutal torture, with the brutality and starvation killing many. Of the 766 known American POWs held during the war, 116 died in captivity before the war ended. Conditions in some camps were so atrocious that in one located in Quan Nam Province, six Americans died between September 1968 and January 1969, including a 19-year old Marine.

Knowing what the POWs faced, the military did everything it could to free the POWs, if it could find them. In October 1966, the US assembled an ad hoc interagency group to look at the problem, becoming known as the "Interagency Prisoner of War Intelligence Committee (IPWIC)" in 1967, and consisting of the military, CIA, FBI, Defense Intelligence Agency (DIA), Department of State, and other agencies as needed.

In theater, *Bright Light* missions searched for POWs in suspected sites in Laos and North Vietnam, including some in enemy-held South Vietnam. Dozens of these raids on suspected POW sites freed American allies but failed to free any American prisoners. The JPRC (Joint Personnel Recovery Center) set up escape and evasion (E&E) networks, conducted continuous Search and Rescue briefings for aircrews, did weekly aerial reconnaissance and evaluations of Selected Areas for Evasion (SAFE) pickup points, delivered education on monthly E&E code letters, provided E&E kit for aerial delivery, and dropped over 200 million leaflets offering rewards for information on the missing.

American and allied forces captured in South Vietnam, Laos, and Cambodia were held in makeshift jungle camps while awaiting transfer to permanent camps. Search missions, including *Bright Light* MACV-SOG operations, found many South Vietnamese, but never found Americans, often just barely missing them. (USAF)

By 1968, the reward program had resulted in the recovery of nine deceased US personnel, information on 22 prisoners, and four rewards for the assistance and recovery of four live US Army personnel and two live Air Force pilots.

The two operations netted copious quantities of invaluable intelligence on the network of POW sites. Finding where the POWs were held in North Vietnam through overhead surveillance flights was near impossible given the dense vegetation, the rudimentary Vietnamese construction, and the small number of prisoners at each site. Captured enemy fighters routinely reported captured Americans and POW camps but were often missing key details or were hard to verify. For example, an April 1968 DIA interrogation report of a South Vietnamese man reported that a "small thatched hut was being used by VC [Viet Cong] to detain PWs [POWs] and civilian suspects" and a March 1968 interrogation reported that a "PW camp consisted of two houses, evacuated by their former owners … Thirty of the PWs died of wounds, sickness, or were killed."

MACV-SOG paid particular attention to one item of interest. Approximately 30 miles west of Hanoi, near Son Tay, was supposedly a compound holding POWs. The DIA (Defense Intelligence Agency) first learned of a camp at Son Tay in September 1967. According to General Jack Singlaub, MACV-SOG, under his command, studied this compound in 1968 for a possible mission, and planning continued through his tour and on to the next commander. While nothing came of the information, Son Tay was a location to watch.

Information continued to come in from different sources indicating POWs were in the area. Among the reams of sometimes sketchy data was a February 2, 1970 DIA report detailing the interrogation of a captured North Vietnamese Army (NVA) soldier who reported he had been a cook in a POW camp near Son Tay. His report was tantalizingly detailed and was somewhat credible, despite some ridiculous assertions. The camp, according to him, consisted of two rows of buildings, each about 100m long, holding 40 to 50 prisoners, probably all Americans, but possibly some Australians. He described the prisoners wearing green uniforms without emblems, wearing rubber sandals, and appeared to be "big and fat" and in good spirits. The POWs each lived in a separate cell of about 3 x 4m long containing a bed, desk, chair, and electric light. POWs were responsible for cleaning their own cells and fed three times a day on pork, bread, and vegetables. The prisoners received cigarettes and soft drinks. The camp had some recreational items such as ping pong tables and a volleyball court and some musical instruments. Amazingly, the source claimed the POWs had some freedom of movement outside the camp and

POW Camp Locations and Route Packs

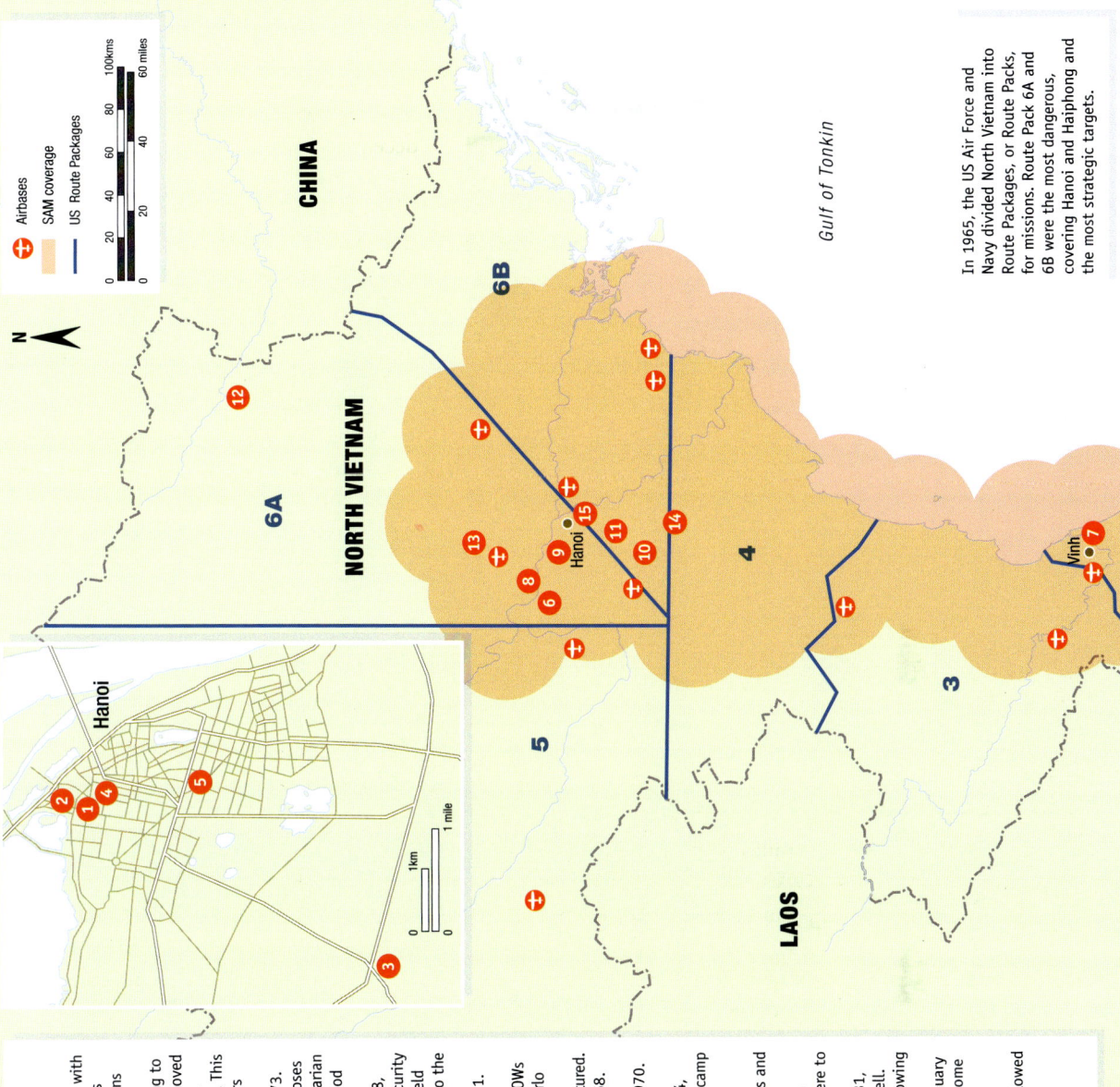

1 Alcatraz (Ministry of National Defense). Americans held October 25, 1967 to August 17, 1970. Known as the worst prison in North Vietnam with underground cells and little ventilation. The defiant group of Americans known as 'The Alcatraz Gang' included several future American politicians including vice-presidential candidate Vice Admiral James Stockdale.

2 Dirty Bird. Americans held June 25, 1967 to October 25, 1967. Hoping to deter American strikes on the powerplant, several dozen POWs were moved into it. Black dust filled the air and covered everything in this prison.

3 Zoo (Cu Loc). Americans held September 10, 1965 to March 29, 1973. This camp took on the name "zoo" because the gaps in the prison cell doors made it easy for prison guards to see inside.

4 Plantation (Citadel). Americans held June 6, 1967 to March 16, 1973. A cleaned-up prison the North Vietnamese used for propaganda purposes to fool pro-North Vietnam anti-war protestors, international humanitarian organizations, and diplomats into thinking the POWs were held in good conditions in compliance with international law.

5 Hanoi Hilton (Hoa Lo). Americans held August 11, 1964 to March 28, 1973. Largest of the prison compounds, the former French central security headquarters and prison in Hanoi. Future senator John McCain was held here following his capture after he was shot down. It was divided into the compounds of Heartbreak, New Guy Village, Vegas, and Unity.

6 Briarpatch (Xom Ap Lo). Americans held August 31, 1965 to July 1971. Located 35 miles west of Hanoi and built to take in the overflow of prisoners from Hanoi Hilton. Conditions were some of the worst with POWs suffering severe malnutrition. An American civilian Merchant Marine, Arlo Gay, was held here after his capture on April 30, 1975 and released in September 1976. He had tried escaping in July 1976, only to be recaptured.

7 Portholes (Bao Cao). Americans held Sept, 1967 to August 28, 1968. This camp had very small cells.

8 Camp Hope (Son Tay). Americans held May 23, 1968 to July 14, 1970. Target of the largest POW rescue attempt.

9 Camp Faith (Dan Hoi). Americans held July 14, 1970 to November 24, 1970. A new facility built about 15 miles from Son Tay, it was a large camp for 200 POWs and had a reputation for better treatment of POWs.

10 Farnsworth, D-1 (Duong Ke). Americans held August 29, 1968 to November 25, 1970. Officers were segregated into black-painted cells and POW treatment was more brutal than at other locations.

11 Skid Row, Hughey, K-77 (Ban Liet). Americans held July 7, 1968 to January 1, 1973. Uncooperative POWs from Hanoi Hilton were sent here to stay in filthy conditions.

12 Dogpatch (Loung Lang). Americans held May 14, 1972 to January 31, 1973. This camp would hold up to 20 POWs crammed into a single cell. The camp was located in the Chinese North Vietnam buffer zone, knowing it was off-limits for US military operations.

13 Mountain Camp (K-49). Americans held December 12, 1971 to January 28, 1973. Situated in the hills near Hanoi, this camp actually had some furniture in cells.

14 Rockpile, Stonewall (Noi Coc). Americans held June 21, 1971 to February 14, 1973. This camp was known to be lenient and POWs allowed to interact with each other.

15 Countryside (Xom De). Americans held January 16, 1973 to February 6, 1973.

had good relations with the camp staff. DIA analysts believed the location and physical description of the camp were accurate, but the rest of the details were incredible.

Gathering all these reports was another secretive group tasked with locating the POWs. At the 1127th Field Activities Group, located at Fort Belvoir, Virginia, personnel combed through the reports and reconnaissance photographs. Soon, they zeroed in on two camps outside of Hanoi – Ap Lo and Son Tay. In studying the photos – the compound at Son Tay seemed to be expanding, including the recent construction of a probable guard tower in the northwest corner – tell-tale signs of prisoners emerged. On April 1, DIA notified CINCPAC that Son Tay "has been confirmed as a currently operational POW camp for US POWs" with up to 55 prisoners according to eyewitness accounts. Intelligence indicated up to six prisoners were routinely assigned to a work detail outside of the camp at Ba Vi. DIA based its conclusion partially on a written message given to a North Vietnamese source which said: "REQMANORSAREPKMTBAVI" or "Request man or SAR [search and rescue] east peak Mt Ba Vi."

The CIA was also picking up indications of a POW camp in Son Tay. An August 1967 memo said a source in 1965 had identified two American prisoners near Son Tay possibly in transit to Hanoi. On February 24, 1970, an internal CIA document stated the "probable prison camp at Son Tay is being enlarged." On May 13, a CIA memo detailed photo analysis showing construction of irrigation canals near the camp from September to November 1969.

Analysts convinced Brigadier General James R. Allen, Deputy Chief of Staff for Plans and Operations that POWs were in Son Tay. On May 25, 1970, General Allen, and the key figures of the 1127th met with Brigadier General Donald D. Blackburn, the Special Assistant for Counterinsurgency and Special Activities (SACSA) to the Chairman of the Joint Chiefs of Staff

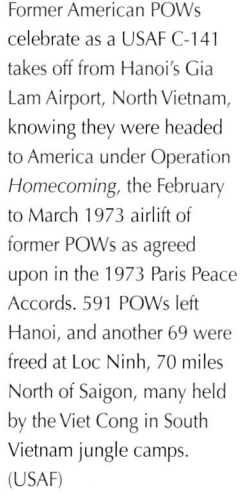

Former American POWs celebrate as a USAF C-141 takes off from Hanoi's Gia Lam Airport, North Vietnam, knowing they were headed to America under Operation *Homecoming*, the February to March 1973 airlift of former POWs as agreed upon in the 1973 Paris Peace Accords. 591 POWs left Hanoi, and another 69 were freed at Loc Ninh, 70 miles North of Saigon, many held by the Viet Cong in South Vietnam jungle camps. (USAF)

(JCS) to outline a rescue plan. The plan called for rescue helicopters with an Army Special Forces contingent to be based 105 miles west of Son Tay at a CIA station in northern Laos. If approved, a covert flight would insert US military agents around Ba Vi to gather information on how often, when, and how many POWs from Son Tay were assigned to work in Ba Vi. If the agent spotted the prisoners and conditions were ripe for rescue, he would send a radio signal and within an hour rescuers would whisk the six POWs away.

Generals Allen and Blackburn liked the idea, but something else was on their minds. The rescue of the POWs was not just about getting them back and boosting morale and the confidence of all American military personnel, especially pilots, but what if the rescue could change the outcome of the war? By 1970, the Paris peace talks had accomplished little. While the US believed it could bomb North Vietnam into submission, both sides knew the American public was weary of the war and would not tolerate the resumption of a bombing campaign, halted since 1968. But the US was not about to just pack up and leave POWs behind. In the calculus of war, if America rescued the POWs, the leaders in Hanoi would lose their only real bargaining chip. Furthermore, the sight of rescued, emaciated, and tortured POWs might turn international opinion against Hanoi, which had, by this point, mastered the use of POWs for propaganda purposes, skillfully allowing only public images of healthy-looking POWs and Red Cross visits to POW facilities cleaned up in advance. General Blackburn proposed getting all the POWs out of Son Tay.

Flabbergasted, the briefers had several misgivings. A larger-scale operation would slow planning down, delay a rescue, put more personnel at risk, and make the mission inordinately more complicated. Just as importantly, the war was highly political. A mission of this size would require Presidential approval which was unlikely. As part of the bombing halt of 1968, President Johnson forbade the military from mounting special operations, agent insertions, or even resupplying covert teams in North Vietnam. Handlers abandoned nine of these Controlled American Sources (CAS) teams leaving them to fend for themselves. A large rescue was out of the question.

Blackburn, however, was not so sure. When the briefing was over, accompanied by Colonel E.E. "Ed" Mayer, head of the Special Operations Division within SACSA, he marched directly over to see General Earle G. Wheeler, Chairman of the JCS. Wheeler listened intently to the initial idea of quickly launching a small rescue of the six men at Mount Ba Vi, increasing the odds of failure. The second proposal astounded Wheeler – rescue all the POWs in Son Tay. Coming on the heels of the April 29 US invasion of Cambodia, Wheeler doubted an operation of this size – he thought it would take battalions to pull it off – was politically viable. Blackburn assured him it was possible with a small Special Forces team. Wheeler gave in to Blackburn but wanted his successor, Admiral Thomas H. Moorer, briefed. Wheeler went to his superior, Air Force Lieutenant General John Vogt, the Joint Chief's Director of Operations, for a feasibility study of the mission by June 1.

ORIGINS

Polar Circle and the Planning Phase

The feasibility plan became "*Polar Circle*," an innocuous code name that would throw off anyone not part of the operation. Analysts had been pouring over high-level SR-71 photographs and other tidbits of information coming in about Ap Lo and Son Tay. Photo interpreters calculated there were at least 50, possibly up to 100, POWs in Son Tay. Soon, analysts and planners calculated that the idea of inserting an agent around Mount Ba Vi and mounting a small rescue was not worth the risk of compromise. If things went wrong, it would end any hope of mounting a larger rescue in the future. At the same time, the opposite was true and the conclusion the same – if the mission was successful, any hope of mounting a larger rescue in the future would be slim, as the element of surprise had been lost.

One option considered was launching from CIA sites on the Laotian border 105 miles away, which were close enough to negate the need for a complicated in-flight refueling plan. The plan called for the helicopters to land inside the Son Tay compound, break open the cells, and fly the POWs out. The Laotian gambit had one major flaw. Laos was crawling with North Vietnamese intelligence agents who would undoubtedly pick up preparations for a rescue mission.

Launching out of Thailand looked better. Although further away, the risk of spies was far less. Coming from Thailand, however, would require a larger force and in-flight refueling, a tricky proposition at night and even more dangerous in poor weather. Meteorologists pointed out that the best window of opportunity for a combination of moonlight and good weather conditions was in October.

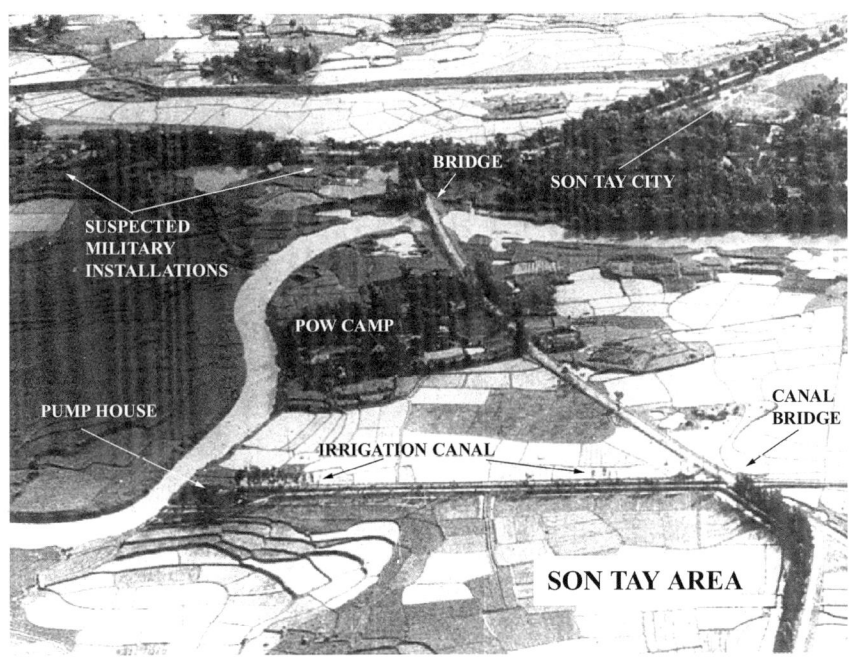

SON TAY AREA

SUSPECTED MILITARY INSTALLATIONS

BRIDGE

SON TAY CITY

POW CAMP

PUMP HOUSE

IRRIGATION CANAL

CANAL BRIDGE

A wide reconnaissance photo of the Son Tay area reveals key terrain and man-made features that mission planners had to account for. Military installations to the north and to the south would be alerted by the sound of the raid and likely send forces to repel the invaders. To prevent this, the commandos would have to quickly move to cover or destroy the bridges to the north and south. Overhead, Skyraiders would help by strafing and bombing targets. (DOD)

The next problem was how to insert the rescuers to achieve maximum surprise, bring about enough firepower to kill the guards, while avoiding harming the prisoners. Among the ideas were the use of High-Altitude Low Opening (HALO) jumps and then movement of the HALO team along the Song Con River. It would then blow holes in the wall and lead the freed prisoners to a landing zone for helicopters to swoop down and rescue them. Another option considered was a static-line air assault with the rescuers fast-roping into the compound. Planners dismissed this notion because of the amount of hovering time needed for the men to drop down, with the full contingent taking up to seven minutes, requiring even more aircraft and firepower to protect the hovering helicopters. Another over-the-top plan included landing helicopters carrying jeeps away from the prison, then using the jeeps to approach the prison, some equipped with battering rams to knock down the gate or wall. A further idea proposed was landing a C-130 on a road next to Son Tay, assaulting the compound, and then flying out via helicopter. With no other options, planners broached the idea of landing one helicopter inside the compound and fighting from the inside out. The compound was not big enough for the entire rescue team to land, but one helicopter could. An initial assault crew could land, kill the guards in the prison cells, while another team landed outside the walls, breached the walls, killed the other hostiles, and helped ferry the POWs out.

To improve the chances of a rescue mission getting in undetected, Blackburn suggested diverting attention away from Son Tay in the west and getting them to focus to the east and Haiphong Harbor. Could the Navy launch strike missions from the Tonkin Gulf? All agreed, this was an idea worth exploring. With a basic conceptual plan in place, albeit with many details to work out, General Blackburn and Mayer briefed General Wheeler

The Joint Chiefs of Staff in January 1970. By then, they knew public support for the war had gone, but Americans were united in their anger over the treatment of the POWs in North Vietnam. In the coming months, they would have to weigh military capabilities, political calculations, and public sentiment when deciding what to do with the intelligence around Son Tay. Left to Right: General John Ryan, Admiral Thomas Moorer, General Earle Wheeler, General William Westmoreland, and General Leonard Chapman. (Getty)

on June 2 who was enthusiastic about the idea. With the key top brass in tune with the plan, Blackburn and Mayer headed to the "tank" to brief the JCS on June 5. To their amazement, Blackburn and Mayer received the go-ahead from the JCS to put together feasibility plans for a rescue mission of the POWs at Son Tay and Ap Lo. Time was running out, and they had just started.

For the detailed intelligence, the planners would utilize the Defense Intelligence Agency, still in its infancy, having been formed in 1961. With arm twisting and bureaucratic maneuvering, *Polar Circle* secured the full cooperation of the CIA. *Polar Circle* planners would get the use of SR-71 reconnaissance aircraft, Teledyne Ryan "Buffalo Hunter" reconnaissance drones, and McDonnel Douglas RF-4 reconnaissance Phantoms.

On July 10, Blackburn briefed the JCS, now presided over by Admiral Moorer, who had replaced General Wheeler after his well-deserved retirement. Moorer, wracked by the political considerations of the war, also agreed with Blackburn on the necessity of rescuing the POWs. "If we could get 50 or 60 of those boys back and let them tell in their own words what had happened to them, it would throw a new light on the character of the North Vietnamese."[1]

By July 10, DIA had learned the camp at Ap Lo was empty, which was some relief, making the decision easier. Moving on two camps would have been incredibly risky. Instead, they could concentrate on Son Tay, which DIA had determined held 61 POWs. Next, the question was what would happen to the POWs if the mission failed or even to the POWs in other camps if the mission failed or succeeded. Would the North Vietnamese treat the POWs worse? The CIA and a Vietnam specialist on the National Security Council concluded that a rescue attempt would be "the greatest thing America could

1   Schemmer, 65

do" for all the prisoners. They speculated their treatment would immediately improve and others speculated an increase in security, but retaliation against the remaining POWs was a concern. The CIA, in a July 1, 1970 memo to General Blackburn, doubted that the Hanoi government would take "any new dramatic external steps whether the operation was successful or not. Should the state of the Paris negotiations continue to be roughly the same in October 1970, as it is now, it is also unlikely they would break off the talks." However, the Communists could retaliate with the "execution of any of the attack party captured, but we do not feel that this would be extended to include prisoners themselves. It would seem unlikely that they would reverse themselves by resurrecting the specter of war crimes."

Brigadier General Donald Blackburn listens intently to a briefing with Colonel "Bull" Simons behind him. Blackburn, as the Special Assistant for Counter Insurgency and Special Activities, personally led the design of the mission and selection of personnel. (DOD)

Blackburn's new plan was risky – it called for a UH-1 "Huey" helicopter to land in the middle of the compound with an assault team. The rescuers would hit the POW cellblocks before the guards could react, with flares dropped by the helicopter blinding the guards. Outside the south wall, larger helicopters would land with the rest of the raiders who would blow a hole in the wall and guide or carry the prisoners out. Another contingent of Americans would kill the guards in the prison's support area and establish blocking positions on a road east of the compound to prevent reinforcements from reaching the camp. In all, Blackburn calculated he needed 50 Green Berets to be in and out of the camp in less than 26 minutes.

A number of NVA forces were around Son Tay, including the 12th Infantry Regiment 6 miles away, an artillery school, an army supply depot about 20 minutes away, and about 500 troops of an air defense unit about 25 minutes away by daylight. One more facility was in the vicinity, but its exact nature was unclear. Labeled the "Secondary School" it looked like a smaller version of the Son Tay camp and was about 500yds south. Whatever was there exactly, planners did not regard it as an immediate threat.

As the JCS discussed the operation, its members asked pointed and logical questions, wanting clarifying details on enemy locations, plans if the rescuers took casualties, and other questions the briefers could answer. The JCS finally approved the plan, setting in motion one of the most incredible raids in US military history. Now, the big question was who would lead it? Blackburn and Mayer had to find someone crazy enough to fly deep into North Vietnam to conduct a rescue mission against incredible odds. One name came up over and over.

The Legendary Arthur "Bull" Simons Assembles his Men

Born on June 28, 1918, Arthur D. Simons was 52 years old as the Son Tay raid planning ramped up. For a US Army officer Special Forces soldier

On April 27, 1973, Colonel Arthur "Bull" Simons, in his Class A uniform, and his wife, ride along the San Francisco parade route honouring his men and former POWs. San Francisco was the epicenter of anti-war protests at the height of the war, but nearly everyone cared about the POWs and celebrated their release under Operation *Homecoming*. (National Archives)

that was old, but "Bull" was not a normal officer. By 1970, he was a colonel and was well known among the Special Forces, having participated in the daring January 30, 1945 raid on the Japanese POW camp at Cabanatuan, Philippines, that freed over 500 prisoners, most of which were American. In the early 1960s, Simons led a team to secretly train the Laotian military and later conducted raids in North Vietnam with MACV-SOG. In 1966, he returned to Fort Bragg, North Carolina for a tour with the XVIII Airborne Corps.

This is where Blackburn and Mayer found him on July 13, 1970.

Simons, fully recovered from a stroke he had suffered years previously, looked, and felt, great to Blackburn. Blackburn and Mayer knew that Simons, the professional soldier, and someone who was no-nonsense and not interested in the political games necessary to be a general, was the man to lead the mission. Blackburn only asked, without mentioning North Vietnam or prisoners or any other details, if Simons would be interested in heading up a secret mission that could be "rough." Simons, without hesitation, responded, "Hell, yes."

With Simons on board, they needed a training site. The two obvious options were the 130,698 acres of Fort Bragg, North Carolina, or the 464,980 acres of the Air Force Special Warfare Center at Eglin Air Force Base in the panhandle of Florida. While Blackburn favored Fort Bragg and a special area he picked out, the commander said no because it housed the Personnel Records Section and the Judge Advocate General. Despite Blackburn again explaining the importance of the site for an extremely sensitive mission, the answer was still no. Blackburn did not have time to play games. Eglin would be it.

With the planning tempo picking up pace, "*Polar Circle*" became "*Ivory Coast*" and forces assembled for the mission became known as the "Joint Contingency Task Group" (JCTG).

Air Force Brigadier General Leroy J. Manor, who had in February 1970 taken command of the US Air Force Special Operations at Eglin Air Force Base in Florida, was named as overall commander with Simons serving as the JCTG Deputy Commander and leader of the mission on the ground.

Manor and Simons flew to the Pentagon for a briefing on the raid proposal, which they enthusiastically supported, and the Pentagon promised all the support they needed as their mission was of the highest priority for the JCS. Air Force Chief of Staff, General John D. Ryan, gave Manor a letter ordering all Air Force commanders to give Manor their full support with no questions asked. Other agencies including the DIA, CIA, National Security Agency (NSA), and the National Reconnaissance Office would lend their assistance. The NSA had countless hours of recorded enemy transmissions but lacked any information about POWs. All the intel would have to be from photographic reconnaissance and any tidbits of information from other sources.

With minimal intelligence at this point, other than knowing there were 61 POWs at Son Tay, Manor and Simons faced another problem – the short timetable. There were only a few months to plan the mission in detail, assemble a team, conduct training, move all assets into place, and conduct the mission. A large-scale rescue by helicopter was unheard of and the men would be inventing everything from the equipment to the tactics entirely from scratch.

On August 8, they would reconvene for five days of detailed planning. Meanwhile, a special security team would develop cover stories and work out counterintelligence plans. In the middle of the Cold War, if the Chinese or the Soviets picked up any indication of a rescue, they would alert the North Vietnamese who would either prepare better defenses or move the prisoners. Simultaneously, another team would head to Eglin to pick out training sites for the newly chosen raiders to begin training by September 9 and be ready to launch by late October.

General Manor's first choice as Air Deputy was Colonel Warner A. Britton, who jumped at the chance to participate in the raid. Manor allowed Britton to then select the key helicopter crews to insert the men. Britton grabbed Lieutenant Colonel John Allison; Colonel Herbert E. Zehnder; and Major Frederic M. "Marty" Donohue.

Bull Simons immediately knew who he wanted for the ground forces. They were Lieutenant Colonel Elliott P. "Bud" Sydnor to serve as his overall deputy, and Captain Richard J. "Dick" Meadows to lead the compound assault team. Lieutenant Colonel Joseph R. Cataldo showed up unannounced, and convinced Simons to take him as the mission doctor.

Captain Dick Meadows, like Simons, was already a legend in the Special Forces community. Born on June 16, 1931, Meadows had joined the US Army in 1946 when he was only 15 years old. He got his first taste of combat in 1950 in Korea. In 1960, Meadows continued to hone his experience by participating in an exchange program with the elite British Special Air Service (SAS). After passing the rigorous SAS training, he deployed with the SAS in the Omani Civil War. Meadows volunteered in 1965 for Vietnam as part of the MACV-SOG. His missions included numerous deep reconnaissance missions in Laos and North Vietnam and so impressed General Willam Westmoreland, that Meadows received a battlefield commission in 1967.

In July 1970, Meadows received a call from the Pentagon letting him know General Blackburn of the SACSA had personally selected him for a mission. Upon Meadows' arrival in Washington, his old commanding officer, Bull Simons, was there to greet him. Meadows knew whatever reason he was in Washington it had to be important if Blackburn and Simons were involved. He was surprised when Simons let him in on the closely guarded secret – the US

Blueboy Assault Group under Captain Dick Meadows had the riskiest and most important mission of all – to crash land *Banana 1*, an HH-3, in the middle of the camp and then assault the prison cells, freeing the prisoners. Earlier ideas of fast-roping into the compound were deemed too risky and time consuming. Instead, planners counted on the audacity and ferocity of this assault to take the prison guards completely by surprise. (USAF)

was going into North Vietnam to rescue POWs. Meadows did not hesitate to say yes.

Through quiet word of mouth via company first sergeants and simple messages in Fort Bragg's daily bulletins, Colonel Simons recruited the rest of the raiders. Simons told the men assembled at a base theater that he was looking for volunteers for a moderately hazardous duty, with no extra pay for temporary duty. It was a simple talk, but Simons' legendary status in the Special Forces community meant every one of them knew it was going to be a daring mission, whatever it was. He told them if they were interested, think it over, and be back at 1300hrs. The gathered men could only guess what the mission was. From terrorist attacks in Europe, to the steady drumbeat of war in the Middle East, to brushfire wars in Africa, to tensions between India and Pakistan, to Fidel Castro, the thorn in America's side, to the wars in Southeast Asia, the mission could be anywhere. Several hundred returned.

Over the next three days, Simons and Cataldo interviewed those still interested. All had excellent records, but he and Cataldo still screened out some for various medical and psychological reasons including those with pregnant wives – their minds might be elsewhere during the mission – or if they did not look like they could carry a POW out on their shoulders. Some questions gauged applicants' mental and physical attributes and attitudes, but were always framed around a geographical locale that did not give away the true destination. If the applicants compared notes afterwards, they surely wondered why some had been asked about welding, skiing, others about scuba diving, and others about desert survival. The 15 officers and 82 enlisted men finally selected knew only to report to Auxiliary Field No. 3 at Eglin Air Force Base (AFB) by September 3.

Manor personally called on men he already knew. Like Simons, he could only be vague about what he was up to. He only told them it was highly classified, it was risky, but it was a good operation. Manor excused those that did not want to participate based solely on the limited information he provided. He did not reveal details of the raid unless the men volunteered and even then, only a select few received more details. Major Thomas R. Waldron, a veteran of SAR missions, found out he was going after he arrived in Eglin for what was supposed to be an instructional rotation. Waldron was asked if he would go on a highly dangerous and classified mission, where details would be forthcoming. Manor would get the aircrews and support personnel for two Combat Talons (one from Detachment 2, 1st Special Operations Wing (SOW) from Pope AFB and one from 7th Special Operations Squadron (SOS) at Ramstein Airbase, West Germany) and five A-1E Skyraiders from Tactical Air Command; finally Military Airlift Command provided five HH-53s, a UH-1, and an HH-3.

A reconnaissance photo of the Son Tay POW camp in the fall of 1970, before the raid. Photo interpreters spent hours analysing the photos looking for troop dispositions and defenses. The photos allowed for incredibly detailed mock-ups, models, and planning of the mission. Unfortunately, for all the scrutiny, uncertainty remained as to whether any POWs were there. (DOD)

SON TAY

INITIAL STRATEGY

Operation *Ivory Coast*: Training and Preparation for the Rescue

On August 8, there was sufficient progress to generate a JCS message for the unified and specified commands around the world advising them that Manor and Simons were now in command of "Joint Contingency Task Group" for "Operation *Ivory Coast*" and the JCS expected full cooperation.

In August, planners tasked Detachment 2 of Combat Knife, a C-130 unit formed in 1969 to pick up personnel in escape and evasion actions within enemy territory, to provide an aircraft and crew to the Son Tay rescue operation and Detachment 2's first combat mission. In Europe, the 7th SOS sent a combat-ready crew back to the US for a mission. The crew, requested by name, meant pulling them from different aircraft for an unknown mission. Upon arrival in Eglin, General Manor said they had an extremely dangerous mission for them, but only if they volunteered. All accepted.

As the personnel roster began taking shape, Manor selected training facilities at Eglin. Eglin's Auxiliary Field Number 3 would be perfect, not only for its capabilities but in a little bit of historical symbolism, it was the field that the Doolittle Raiders had trained on in World War II to bomb Japan in their famous raid that shook Japanese leadership to the core. The training location consisted of six barracks, classrooms, one secure building for the Tactical Operations Center (TOC), a Post Exchange and snack bar, a theater, mess facilities, and a motor pool. The men began

The fantastically detailed model of Son Tay, "Barbara," not only showed the camp structures and defenses, but also showed the terrain to factor into planning. While the river on the west side adjacent to the wall meant a ground assault or landing zone (LZ) from that side was impossible, the flat, clear farming terrain on the south side presented an LZ for another group of raiders to assault from that direction. (DOD)

converting their new home into a headquarters and training facility, establishing a secure TOC building with three rolls of concertina barbed wire, giving only one entrance, and installing field communications. The TOC, even on an AFB, and surrounded by barbed wire, required men on guard duty around the clock, further adding to the mystery of where the men were going.

The biggest dilemma was how to construct a mockup of the target site. The commanders were not about to launch a mission this risky based on map exercises and sand tables alone. The problem was that the Soviets were closely monitoring US military bases and satellites crisscrossed the skies watching for anything unusual at bases around the world. If they spotted the mockup and figured out what the Americans were up to, they would alert their North Vietnamese allies.

After considering the options of how to construct a mockup but needing to hide it before each Soviet satellite passed overhead, they had an ingenious solution. The group ordered 1,500yds of target cloth and 710 6ft two-by-four pieces of lumber to make outlines of the walls and corridor of the unidentified target. An observer might notice billowing white cloth in the Florida woods but would not know its purpose. Fearful of satellites or overhead flights picking up the target, the men planned to assemble and dissemble the mockup for each training session, even covering the holes used to fix the two-by-four posts to hide the outline of the mockup. Analysts determined there was no way the mockup and concealment looked like a POW compound, negating the need for constantly assembling and disassembling the mock camp.

Intelligence on the POWs and Son Tay

As planning ramped up, reconnaissance and analysis of the camp and surrounding area intensified, looking at prisoner activity, troop dispositions and movements, and items that could throw off the plans. For *Ivory Coast*, planners had access to not only SR-71 high-altitude reconnaissance flights, but also Buffalo Hunter reconnaissance drones, developed in the early 1960s. By the time the war was over, 3,455 drone missions overflew North Vietnam with 578 drones lost.

The men continue their practice assaults on the cloth mock up of the Son Tay prison camp under the harsh Florida sun. The temporary nature of the fake camp enabled the men to quickly disassemble it and hide it from the prying eyes of the Soviet satellites or others not in on the secret mission. Security concerns drove much of the planning and the men wouldn't know until the day of the raid exactly where they were going. (USAF)

The range of the drones was never sufficient to ground launch them from South Vietnam and the Air Force rejected the idea of using them off the ships after failed tests. To get close, the Air Force had to locate the DC-130 launch and control aircraft in Bien Hoa, South Vietnam, and U-Tapao, Thailand, with recovery CH-3s located in Da Nang, South Vietnam, and Nakhon Phanom, Thailand. Further control officers were located at Monkey Mountain in Da Nang. Despite being in Vietnam and in

A DC-130 approaching the launch point for a mission over North Vietnam. First appearing in Vietnam in 1964, a Teledyne Ryan "Buffalo Hunter" drone is carried by a DC-130 to the aerial launch point. Some 3,455 drone missions were flown during the war, with 578 lost. Seven of these flights took them over Son Tay, but it wasn't until after the mission that the DC-130 crews knew why they were sending the drones in that direction. (Air Commando Association)

the 7th Air Force operational space, SAC headquarters in Omaha, Nebraska, held actual operational authority and control of the drones.

With no defensive capabilities, the top-secret missions required complete radio silence, low-level flying, and launching in the pre-dawn darkness. Intended for higher-altitude flights, drones had navigation and photography instrumentation calibrated with that in mind. In September, drone operators received a set of coordinates needing further photo coverage by the Buffalo Hunters. Command told the drone operators to modify their tactics to further deny advance warning that drones were about to appear overhead at this target to make sure all the drones made it home. To further conceal the drone launches and flights, the DC-130 control and launch aircraft, normally escorted by fighters so close to North Vietnam, found themselves flying alone, a risky proposition for the crews given that in 1970 540 MIGs went after the drones.

The only thing pilots and drone operators knew was that they were looking at "positive identification of the enemy order of battle." Meanwhile, the 7th Air Force in Saigon maintained Tactical Air Command over the RF-4 reconnaissance Phantoms and RF-101 reconnaissance Voodoos. Drones flew over Son Tay seven times between September and late October, with two shot down by anti-aircraft fire and four others failing due to mechanical or weather issues. One final Buffalo Hunter mission pushed the limits of revealing something was in the works. The drone was supposed to fly just barely over the walls of the compound and take detailed pictures. Unfortunately, it banked too soon and took only worthless photos of the horizon beyond Son Tay.

Not willing to risk further low-level flights revealing a raid in planning, the rest of the reconnaissance flights were tasked to SR-71s out of Kadena AFB, Okinawa, and the film sent to DIA photo interpreters at SAC's 67th Reconnaissance Technical Squadron in Yokoto AFB, Japan, which would then send the photos back to Washington. The last photographs from

The Redwine Command Element after one of the many dress rehearsals. They are wearing the standard uniform of the raid – green jungle fatigues, patrol caps, and goggles. Before the raid, the uniforms would be sanitized with patches, ranks, and name tags removed. To clear obstacles, the men relied on explosives and a chainsaw and axe for good measure. (USAF)

OPPOSITE
After another night rehearsal in Florida, Colonel Simons discusses the mission with Lieutenant Colonel Joseph Cataldo, the mission's chief medical officer who was to supervise the medical treatment of the freed POWs and mission personnel. The POWs were expected to be in poor health and in shock at being rescued so extensive planning and preparation was made to take care of them mentally and physically at every point from the rescue to the eventual trip to America. (USAF)

the SR-71 on October 3 showed something puzzling. Where were the POWs? The SR-71 and drone reconnaissance showed no significant changes or causes of concern. That is until one analysis pointed out that, since June 6, the camp was "less active."

With the air reconnaissance proving futile for immediate intelligence, human intelligence (HUMINT) sources were essential. One was a CAS insert, a program grudgingly restarted under President Nixon. This CAS insert would find a way to travel through Son Tay, on a bicycle, and in an amazing coincidence, would have to fix a flat tire right outside of the compound. The asset was to be in and out of Son Tay well before the mission. There is some debate as to whether the actual asset was inserted, but in any case, no intelligence came from the idea. Another HUMINT asset was a North Vietnamese official, Nguyen Van Hoang, in the Enemy Proselyting Office. Through clandestine means, he would smuggle out information about Son Tay and other POW camps.

Bureaucracy, Support, and Logistics

Before any of the real training could begin, there were a host of details and tasks to work out. Logistically, the mission was a headache for producing equipment. At Auxiliary Field 3, the Logistics Plans Branch of the 3246th Test Wing coordinated the organization of billeting, mess, laundry, munitions storage, telephone lines, transportation, helicopter maintenance, medical facilities, and civil engineering capabilities. When official supply sources did not have the right equipment, the men went to local stores to purchase needed equipment.

Personnel bought bolt cutters and acetylene torches through a variety of civilian and military channels to cut various locks on the prison cells. For example, they found the Air Force Fire Fighters had the best bolt cutters and bought the torches and six chainsaws on the local market. The list was endless and supply sergeants scoured all government and private sources to outfit the team with kit including electrical head lamps, E&E kits, and 35mm cameras. Raiders purchased bullhorns to announce their presence to the POWs. The Special Operations Force at Hurlburt Field, Florida, provided rucksacks patterned after Vietnamese designs. Ear protection, goggles, flying gloves, six cut-fire axes, and a 14ft scaling ladder all eventually found their way to the special base at Eglin now humming with activity, even if some of it had to be procured from Sears Roebuck. Civilian 12-gauge shotguns found their way into the inventory as they were superior to the military ones.

Colt Arms Company provided 250 30-round magazines for the M16s and CAR-15s, but the standard ammo pouch on the US Load Bearing Equipment (LBE) only held 20-round magazines. To solve that, they used empty Claymore mine bags. Modified rucksacks carried increased loads and specialized equipment. The men even received special custom-made weapons slings, all individually tailored.

One of the most important pieces of equipment obtained was the "Singlepoint" aiming device. With the assault force moving rapidly through the camp at night, the raiders would need accurate fire to hit the guards and avoid endangering the prisoners. Although they were all skilled marksmen, they had to be perfect shots for this mission. The solution came in the form of a civilian device sold for $49.95 that was a red dot pointed at the target, appearing as green at night. Instead of aiming through iron sites, the shooter simply pointed the dot from the light mounted on their weapon. No need to assume formal firing positions or close an eye to aim. Meadows had come across the device at a small arms conference in June 1970 and after seeing it advertised by ArmaLite, Inc. in California, Bull Simons told him to purchase them. The sights increased bullseyes and shot groupings but did not stay mounted tightly. The solution was again expedient – use of lots of black electrician's tape.

Overall, given the short time frame allowed, it was an impressive achievement to get all the specialized equipment, but it taxed to the limit the one supply officer and two supply sergeants assigned to the mission.

The night-time mission required countless night-time full dress rehearsals in Florida. This Green Beret carries a CAR-15 outfitted with the Singlepoint sight and has the red lens in his goggles. A small radio is on his web gear. For the mission, the men would wear sanitized jungle fatigues without ranks, name tags, or unit patches. (USAF)

POW Needs After the Rescue

As planning and training progressed, attention turned to caring for the POWs, whose mental and physical condition would be uncertain. No one expected the POWs to be healthy, rather likely very weak, needing assistance to move from their cells to the helicopters, and afflicted with different illnesses and injuries. Could all the POWs survive the mental and physical shock of the rescue? The Air Force and Navy reviewed plans for the treatment of a substantial number of POWs as well as the medical facilities in Thailand, especially at Udorn Royal Thai Air Force Base (RTAFB).

Medical personnel studied nine previously freed POWs and developed a profile listing expected health problems likely facing the Son Tay POWs. Based on the data, the raiders figured that, pre-internment, the average POW was 171lbs, 33 years old, and 70in tall. In captivity, the POWs would have lost 20 percent of their body weight. Data from World War II indicated that the average weight lost was 32 percent. POWs freed in World War II suffered from malnutrition, skin disease, respiratory disease, old and recent wounds or injuries, and other diseases.

Medical planners estimated that of the 61 POWs, 25 would have malaria, 35 would have intestinal parasites, 40 would suffer from malnutrition, four would have goiter, 12 peripheral neuritis, 15 active dysentery, and 12 active tuberculosis.

According to medical personnel, the POW, kept in dimly lit rooms, would have had little physical exercise, and heard only limited noise. He would have eaten, if fortunate, two meals per day, usually

consisting only of cabbage soup, some bread, and rice, and occasional portions of fish or meat. With the lack of protein and little exercise, most would have muscular atrophy, and barely be able to stand or walk, let alone run to a helicopter. Lesions would be visible on the mouth. Swelling in the neck area and tongue would also be visible, making some of them barely able to speak, except in slurred, slow, speech. They may complain their feet burn and may bruise easily. Psychologically, many would have given up hope of rescue or of ever seeing their families again. Most would barely have the will to survive day-to-day. During the rescue, the realization that American forces were there to take them home would be shocking and paralyzing for some. They may only be able to manage a weak smile, bereft of cheering or excitement upon liberation and may cry.

At the Army Natick Laboratories in Massachusetts, planners came up with specialized medical kits for the POWs. Personnel made specially devised olive-drab sneakers with high-rise eyelets and reinforced sponge insoles. Technicians repackaged food rations which included Heinz rice baby food, selected for its palatability and consistency, packaged in plain sealed foil for security reasons. Planners ordered M5 medical kits that included a Duke Inhaler Set for use with Penthrane (a non-flammable inhalation anesthetic agent), Ketamine HCL, scissors, hemostats, many sizes of bandages, and inflatable splints.

Confident of a successful mission, the Army Surgeon General sent 100 pairs of pajamas and bathrobes from Valley Forge Headquarters to Eglin for use by the POWs on their way back to the US.

Training for the Ground Forces

Phase 1 of training focused on land navigation, survival, patrolling and ambush, communications, demolition, weapons, first aid, and rigorous physical training. The men fired countless rounds, zeroing their weapons,

Codenamed "Barbara," this highly detailed $60,000 CIA model was made from extensive photo reconnaissance, so accurate that during the night of the raid, the men felt they had been there before. The model presented the planners with a number of problems – how to assault a walled compound with one side flanked by a river, guard towers, well-built structures, and military quarters next door. But the model gave them an idea – what if the raiders could land inside the compound? (Getty)

and refining their marksmanship, critical to engaging in expected close quarter battles, at night, with friendlies and POWs in proximity. Countless puzzles needed solving – what was the fastest way to eliminate the guards or what was the sequence for searching cell blocks or the best way to withdraw the force once the prisoners were out? Every single day, the men practiced their assault on the mysterious objective. They were to know each other's roles. As they continued the rehearsals, leaders adjusted and modified plans.

Phase 2 consisted of more emphasis on night operations. This training included detailed medical training, treatment of battlefield wounds, and medical care for the POWs. Night firing and target recognition received special emphasis. The men refined or learned new skills in engaging targets from HH-3 and UH-1 helicopters, calling in close air support, conducting room-to-room clearances, immediate action drills, night land navigation, and target surveillance skills.

Phase 3 saw the force intensifying their dress rehearsals to refine techniques and cut down time in the target area. Raiders trained in dangerous live-fire house-to-house fighting. Specific personnel received specialized training on Forward Air Guide procedures to call in air strikes from A-1E Skyraiders, demolition training, chainsaws, and use of acetylene torches. The designated assault group learned to fire from helicopters while landing in the middle of the camp. The assault element practiced cell-clearing and search practice with the Support and Command groups acting as POWs. The men practiced with night vision devices. Finally, it was time to study "Barbara," a $60,000, CIA-built scale model of Son Tay, even using special prisms to see it from the ground perspective and examine the latest reconnaissance photos with a US Air Force photo interpreter available to answer questions.

Under Simons, the training was rigorous, and commanders had to dismiss a few men. Sydnor relieved one raider who did not bring back his heavy acetylene torch after one run through. Another candidate could not keep up with the training pace and dropped out. Meadows had to dismiss a soldier who had had too much to drink and failed to sober up when given a chance.[2]

Worse than the demanding physical training was the secrecy. The only thing most of the men knew was they were going to be assaulting a compound to free prisoners somewhere. "Kept In the Dark, Fed On Horse Shit" along with a cartoon mushroom became the unofficial motto. Trying to keep men motivated under a rigorous training schedule, while telling them little, was tough. Sydnor said "they were seasoned soldiers who felt that we showed a lack of trust in them by not briefing them."[3] For morale, the men enjoyed a bar with its own jukebox and sometimes a band. While young ladies came in occasionally, the men suspected they were Department of Defense (DOD) personnel testing if the men would speak about their mission after a few drinks. None did. The raiders challenged each other to fights, and other ways to blow off steam.[4]

2   Hoe, 115–116
3   Hoe, 114
4   Buckler, 70

Command Sergeant Major Joe Lupyak later described Simons with his ever-present cigar as tough, fair, and big hearted. At one point in the training, Simons gave the men a day off and took them to Fort Walton Beach for cokes and hot dogs, and rain. "We might as well have kept working. It was miserable."[5]

The Air Component Training

While the ground forces practiced their missions, the Air Force training focused on developing new tactics and equipment for the incredibly complex and dangerous mission. To complicate matters, not everyone was privy to the exact destination, and night flights dominated the training. One HH-53 pilot, Major Jay M. Strayer, speculated that the mission was related to the spate of hijackings by terrorist groups and rescuing some high-level government or corporate official and others wondered if the mission was to Cuba, or Africa, or somewhere else.[6] It could be anywhere given the HH-53's capabilities.

For the mission, planners wanted a Task Group composition of two Combat Talon C-130Es to provide navigation to the target area (the C-130Es would pick up the designation MC-130 in 1977). One C-130E would lead the assault force composed of five HH-53s and either one HH-3 or UH-1H. The other would lead the strike force of five A-1Es.

The first bit of equipment added to the C-130E was Forward Looking Infrared (FLIR). Also an additional navigator joined the crew. Helicopters received special Ground Acquisition Responder/Interrogator (GAR/I) beacons for the Combat Talons to track. The FLIR performance was excellent and all C-130Es would receive FLIR systems, improved navigational radar, and inertial navigational capabilities.

The combined formation training was particularly hair-raising, flying at their maximum and minimum speeds through the hilly terrain of northern Alabama and Tennessee to simulate flying into North Vietnam. For the UH-1 and HH-3 helicopters to keep up with the C-130E, the helicopters had to fly at their maximum speeds in the draft position. For the C-130E to slow down enough for the helicopters to stay in formation, the planes had to extend their flaps to 70 percent and fly at only ten knots above their stall out speeds. While the A-1Es could easily keep up with the C-130Es, during turns, the fully loaded, ordnance-heavy A-1Es had difficulty staying in formation.

Major Donohue and Major Waldron, flying *Apple 3*, earned their spot as lead gunship when Simons had them prove their abilities by shooting up a mock target

In December, Brigadier General Leroy J. Manor conducts another press briefing using the CIA model, "Barbara." Manor, a P-47 pilot during World War II with over 72 missions in Europe, also flew 275 combat missions over Vietnam as commander of the 37th Tactical Air Wing in 1968. In February 1970, he took command of the US Air Force Special Operations Command and, within months, the commander of the Joint Contingency Task Group to rescue the Son Tay POWs. (Getty)

5   Robinson, 30
6   Chinnery, 243

24

with no errant rounds striking a nearby white sheet representing the POW holding cell.

New training and procedures accounted for weather disruptions, loss of visual contact among the aircraft, loss of aircraft, blackout conditions, loss of radios, and every other imaginable scenario. Air-to-air and air-to-ground communications with the Skyraiders were fine-tuned. C-130E crews had to master rigging and dropping BLU-27/B firebomb markers, log flares, and firefight simulators to confuse the enemy.

Helicopter crews worked out countless details, refining positions of seats and stretchers; locations of headsets; cleaning up oil spills; weight and balance of on- and off-loading of personnel; safety of personnel in the passenger area; care in handling sharp equipment, making sure personnel did not use aircraft internal wiring and tubes as grab handles. For the helicopter gun crews, they had to contend with muzzle flashes interfering with their Starlight night vision devices and practicing calculations of ground speed and elevation for firing accuracy. Crews disabled or masked all but one external light and minimized the internal lights on the control panel. In the pitch-black conditions, a big concern was if the aircrews would be temporarily blinded by the flares, gunfire, and explosions during the raid.

As training progressed, one of the most iconic aircraft of the Vietnam War – the Huey helicopter – found itself fighting for a spot on the mission. The venerable UH-1 Huey was perfectly suited to land within the confines of the Son Tay compound, but getting there and having the capabilities to perform the mission were another issue. During training, the UH-1 had an extremely challenging time in keeping up with the C-130s in-flight. Attention turned toward the larger HH-3 and the idea of just crash-landing

A formation of a HC-130P tanker, an HH-3 Jolly Green Helicopter, and two A-1 Skyraiders was the epitome of Search and Rescue (SAR) missions during the Vietnam War. Pilots shot down over Vietnam knew SAR missions would come after them, with the would-be rescuers risking their own lives. The Skyraiders would destroy enemy forces searching for the downed pilot while the helicopter would carry them to safety. These same skills and teamwork were essential to the Son Tay plans. (USAF)

it into the compound emerged. If the HH-3 was to take off after the raid it would make the mission more complicated and require more training, the helicopter would have to hover while landing during the most dangerous part of the mission, the lift-off would make it vulnerable to ground fire, and the debris from the rotors would be a distraction and disorienting. Crash-landing and leaving the Huey behind was the best option.

The A-1 Skyraider training resulted in new flight patterns. A-1s could easily keep up with the C-130Es, but when C-130Es banked into a turn, flying at a low speed so the helicopter could keep up, the A-1s had some difficulty keeping formation. A-1s adjusted their flight patterns and tactics to fly circles or S-turns to keep within range of the C-130s. This spread the aircraft out further, increasing the chances of detection, navigational error, and accidents.

To counter this, the plan changed to splitting up the aircraft into an assault and strike force. The assault force would be composed of the helicopters and the strike force would be the fixed wing aircraft, timed to merge with each other at the proper time.

The raiders conducted a full-scale dress rehearsal on October 6. The practice run included a 687-mile low-level flight and firing live ammunition by the ground forces. The simulated rescue went flawlessly, unsurprising given the 1,000 hours of flight time in the weeks before. The men were ready to go and a select group were told the target. Upon hearing where the mission was going, Major Thomas Waldron, copilot of *Apple 3*, was shocked to learn they were flying straight into the hornet's nest where the SAMs and MIGs were responsible for most of the POWs to begin with. "My jaw dropped."[7] he said.

When to Go

Throughout the training, Blackburn, Manor, and Simons wrestled with the question of exactly when to go. They knew the window of opportunity with moonlight, weather, training, and force capabilities was late October through the middle of November. The preferred date was October 21 if approved by the President.

On September 27, Secretary of Defense Lair and JCS Chief Moorer briefed President Richard M. Nixon, while he was on a European trip, and visiting the Sixth Fleet. To Nixon's surprise, just as he was trying to extract America from Vietnam, the men were proposing a raid inside North Vietnam near Hanoi. Nixon agreed with the need for the mission, but he wanted to hear from his National Security Advisor, Henry Kissinger; envoy for the Paris peace talks, David K. Bruce; and his Deputy, Philip C. Habib. During Kissinger's briefing, he asked Bruce and Habib how likely it was for Hanoi to agree to release the prisoners soon. There was almost no chance they said. Hanoi was holding 500 POWs and was not about to give up their only bargaining chip.

International political machinations in the fall were rapidly interfering with mission dates and the White House wanted the raid delayed until

---

7   Waldron, 88

after the weekend of October 24–25 because of the 25th Anniversary celebrations of the United Nations. Also, in October, Nixon's reproachment with the People's Republic of China was picking up steam with various public statements. A rescue mission at this time could enrage the Chinese and undo the behind-the-scenes work of trying to open relations between the two bitter foes. If not approved for November, it would be months before conditions for a raid were good enough.

On October 8, Manor and Simons discussed the mission again with Kissinger and his deputy, Major General Alexander M. Haig. Anticipating a concern of a high enemy-body count, Simons said the rescuers were not going in to just "blow people's heads off" but "anybody who gets in our way is dead." Kissinger approved and said he would take care of any international fallout and enemy casualties were not a concern for the White House. Kissinger raised the obvious, foreboding question of what if the mission failed and some rescuers were captured? Manor pointed out the aircrews had flown hundreds of flight hours and rehearsed the mission 170 times by that point. Kissinger cut off Blackburn's question of what impact the raid would have on the Paris Peace negotiations, saying "That's our worry, not yours." At the end of the briefing, Kissinger said this was the President's call for a mission this dangerous and with severe political consequences.

The mission timetable was slipping with each delay, and other hiccups kept coming up. The Navy was planning to cancel all Barrier Combat Air Patrol (BCAP) flights – radar flights to keep track of MIG activity. Canceling these flights would leave the rescue force blind to where the North Vietnamese were patrolling. Blackburn was able to get those turned back on, but C-130 flights engaged in leaflet drops, Operation *Litterbug*, were keeping enemy air defense systems alert. Blackburn killed a proposed one-day bombing campaign, the first in over two years, because he believed, while it would provide good cover for the mission, it could provoke the enemy into harming the POWs or changing their air defenses.

On November 1, an advance team from the JCTG headed to Thailand. Manor and Simons then went to Saigon to brief the Commander, US Military Assistance Command, Vietnam General Creighton Abrams, his deputy General Lucius Clay, and the 7th Air Force Commanding General, Lieutenant General Welborn Dolvin. This being the first time they had heard of the mission, they were nonetheless impressed by the detailed plan and preparations. Clay, though, did have to ask, "How crazy are you guys?"[8]

There was one more request, based on the Paris talks, to consider delaying the rescue until December, which Blackburn shot down because weather conditions would push the next window months down the road. Besides, to turn it off now with the men at their peak readiness would kill morale,

At the end of a live fire dress rehearsal in Florida on October 6 that included an over 600-mile flight, the raiders confer in the sweltering heat to work out remaining details. They were razor-sharp ready to launch the mission, even if not all of them knew where they were going, as soon as they got the order. They would soon be carefully loading all the gear for the long flight to Southeast Asia. (USAF)

8 Schemmer, 146

take the edge off, and increase chances the raid would leak. On Thursday, November 12, Secretary of Defense Laird wanted one more look at the mission briefing. On November 13, Deputy Assistant for National Security Affairs Alexander Haig sent Kissinger a memo informing him that there might be some weakening of support for the mission, "it is apparent that Secretary Laird and Lieutenant General Robert E. Pursley are having second thoughts on the operation" due to a supposed deal by a Swedish citizen to provide a large ship to bring all POWs to Saigon. Haig advised Kissinger to make it clear to Laird that Laird was the one who first mentioned the raid, and that the President was enthusiastic about the mission and expected Laird "to carry the ball."

On November 18, Admiral Moorer gave his last pitch for the mission to President Nixon, National Security Adviser Kissinger, CIA Director Helms, Secretary of State Rogers, Secretary of Defense Laird, and General Haig. In prepartion for the meeting, Kissinger outlined that not only were the POW rescue mission preparations near ready, but because the North Vietnamese had shot down an unarmed reconnaissance plane around Ban Karai Pass, the US was going to retaliate against anti-aircraft installations and logistics along the border with Laos after the Son Tay raid. Admiral Moorer said, based on the best intelligence available, there were 61 prisoners – 43 Air Force, 14 Navy, and four Marines. If the President approved the mission, General Manor would execute the mission between November 21 and November 25 under the name Operation *Kingpin*.

President Nixon complimented Moorer on the mission details and the obvious arduous work of all involved before asking what was the latest date he could approve. Moorer stressed if not soon, it would be months later before they could take another shot at it. Nixon understood and said it was not a question of if he would approve, but when. Something else worried the President. He wanted to know how many more POWs were going to die if something was not done quickly. A few days earlier, on November 13, the leaders in Hanoi had delivered a list of men to Peace Activists explaining that six men had been killed when their planes were shot down. It was a complete lie. The men were known to be POWs in decent health, originally captured alive, and one of them, Air Force Major Wilmer N. "Newk" Grubb, shot down in 1966, was featured in several Communist publications as a prisoner. The President recalled an earlier briefing that month that had said as many as 28 POWs had died in captivity. Nixon wanted the POWs freed and he expected to welcome them to the White House for Thanksgiving dinner.

The President asked rhetorically, "How could anyone not approve of this?"

President Nixon approved the mission in the afternoon. The next day he hand-wrote a note to Laird, "Regardless of results, the men on this project have my complete backing and there will be no second guessing if the plan fails. It is worth the risk and the planning is superb."

Admiral Thoms H. Moorer was Chief of Naval Operations between 1967 and 1970 and then Chairman of the Joint Chiefs of Staff. Moorer approved the idea of rescuing the POWs and nursed the idea through Washington politics. When President Nixon asked why anyone would volunteer for such a risky mission, Moorer responded, "Sir, we could have had thousands volunteer to go in to help our POWs." (Getty)

THE PLAN

Operation *Kingpin*–Son Tay Camp

Son Tay consisted of two dozen buildings in and outside the walls plus a guard tower, wells, a fishpond, gardens, trees, walls, gates, and even a torture cell.

Planners designated the primary cell blocks as a five series with the main cells thought to be in buildings 5B and 5E. Built around 1969, 5C and 5D were possibly cell blocks, but the raiders were unsure of their purpose. Building 3 was a latrine and building 4 was a warehouse.

Cell block 5B was 55 x 30ft in size and contained six prison cells of approximately 6 x 8ft size and one of 4 x 10ft. It had a steel door and metal window shutters. The inside floors and walls were concrete with walls at least 6in thick. The exterior of 5B was masonry brick covered in concrete. The doors were ¼in steel and painted green. The outside windows had iron bars imbedded in the window sash.

The inside cell doors were steel with small peep slits cut into them at eye level and slots for bowls of food. All the cells had 10ft-high plaster ceilings with electrical wires dangling from them. A concrete platform on the left side of the cells served as a bed. Surprisingly, there were no leg or arm shackles. Cell block 5E had four cells (two 8 x 20ft and two 8 x 8ft) in addition to an 8 x 20ft unsecured common room. Each of the cells had a raised concrete platform to serve as bedding. As with 5B, the

The Son Tay area captured by an SR-71 after the raid. Visible in the south is "Secondary School" military installation, clearly showing how close it was to the POW camp and of similar size. The HH-53s, slightly off course, assuming that was the target, hurriedly changed course upon realizing the error, except for *Apple 1*, which landed next to it, triggering a vicious firefight. (DOD)

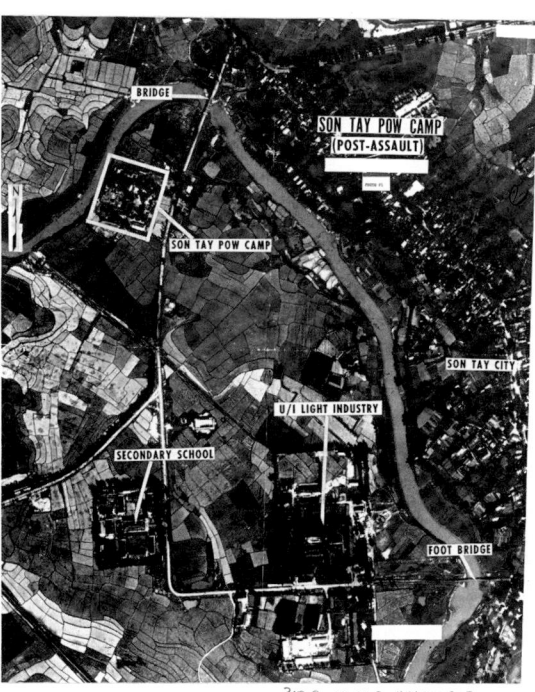

340-B-VN-116-2-114154 USAF

cells had steel doors, swinging outwards, and eye-level peephole slits secured with padlocks. The windows had metal bars and steel screens. The ceiling was 12ft high. No shackles were present.

A walkway led to a 3 x 3ft cubicle with a concrete floor and a drain in the middle to serve as either a latrine or washroom.

Ominously, several hundred yards to the south was another compound of similar dimensions and layout, labeled as a "suspected military installation," next to a river and a similar road, designated the "Secondary School." Simons asked if the pilots and planners were confident that the pilots would not confuse the compounds and land his men at the wrong place. The pilots reassured Simons that the checkpoints and geographic features led to the correct compound. Besides, they said, all they had to do was go to the compound on the left.

When ordered, a specially configured C-130E (*Cherry 1*) to aid in navigation would depart Takhli RTAFB at Nakhon Phanom. Five Close Air Support A-1E Skyraiders (*Peaches 1* through *5*) would join the C-130E and both air components would proceed to a refueling point north of the Plaine de Jarres for aerial refueling. Soon afterwards, a second modified C-130E (*Cherry 2*) would take off from Takhli, overfly Udorn, and proceed to the same refueling point. The assault helicopters, one HH-3 (*Banana*), and five HH-53s (*Apples 1* to *5*) would depart Udorn in time to rendezvous with the refueling aircraft, HC-130Ps (*Lime 1* and *2*).

Cherry 1 and the helicopters would be the first air group with the second air group consisting of the *Cherry 2* and the *Peaches* following ten minutes behind. These two groups would proceed to Laos, entering Vietnam from the west, approaching Son Tay as low as 500ft.

At this time, the US Navy would launch diversionary penetrations of two staggered thrusts toward the coast by squadron-sized forces.

Ten F-4 Phantoms would perform MIG Combat Air Patrol orbits to the northeast and southeast of Hanoi as directed by College Eye EC-121s in orbit over the Gulf of Tonkin. An RC-135 would also be in orbit over the Gulf of Tonkin as an alternate mission command post.

Helping to protect the aircraft would be F-105G Wild Weasels, Firebirds 1–5, flying a SAM suppression mission.

At one-half mile from the objective, *Cherry 1* would signal for the commencement of the assault by ascending to 1,500ft and

releasing flares directly over the prison. *Banana* and the three assault HH-53s, *Apples 1, 2,* and *3,* should then be within 30 seconds of landing at H-hour when the flares ignited.

After dropping flares over the prison, *Cherry 1* would make a right turn and drop firefight simulators southeast of Son Tay city to further confuse enemy forces. *Cherry 1* would then continue to fly to the southwest and drop two firebombs, marker flares, and firefight simulators near an ammunition storage site about 2½ miles southwest of the objective. The firebombs would create a diversion and provide a visible anchor point for two *Peaches* to move forward and orbit the objective about H plus 20 seconds.

Cherry 2 would then proceed west to a point where it could serve as a UHF/DP aid for the *Peaches* and *Apples* when they departed the objective. The *Apples 1* through *3,* upon disembarking their troops at the objective, would move to isolated areas 2½ miles to the northwest where they would land and wait until called back by the Ground Commander after about 20–30 minutes.

The reserve C-130, one A-1, and two reserve HH-53s, *Apples 4* and *5,* tasked with ferrying out the POWs, would turn right out of the line of fight when three minutes away from the objective. They would orbit north of Ba Vi Mountain and the C-130 would hold west of the Black River.

H-hour would be when the lead helicopter, the HH-3, call sign *Banana,* intentionally crash-landed in the courtyard of the objective. The assault group aboard this helicopter, Blueboy, consisting of five section elements (Blueboy Headquarters of three men, with Captain Meadows in command, Blueboy Action Element 1 of four men, Blueboy Action Element 2 of four men, Blueboy Action Element 3 of three men, and the Air Force Element of three men), would secure the inside of the compound. Blueboy Command would blow a hole in the wall near the southwest corner and destroy the HH-3. Blueboy Action 1 would secure the north side of the compound of one guard tower and three buildings with POW cellblocks (5A, designated the "Beer Hall;" 5C, the "Outhouse;" and 5D, the "Stag Bar"). Blueboy Action 2 would clear the largest building (5E, the "Cat House"), clear the southeast of the compound, and cover securing of the east gate. Blueboy Action 3 would attack the east guard tower, cover the POW compound, and free POWs in building 5B, the "Opium Den." The HH-3 *Banana* Air Force crew would move to the south wall and help with keeping the freed POWs organized.

After the men disembarked, the helicopters with the command and support groups would land outside of the compound in cultivated rice fields.

Redwine Security Group, carried by HH-53 *Apple 2,* would land south of guard building 8D. Lieutenant Colonel Sydnor's command party would be located on the east side of building 8E, an animal stable. In addition to a Ground Force Command Group (five men including Lieutenant Colonel Cataldo) and Security Group (two men), would have four security elements. The Security Group would secure the south wall and help with the movement of POWs to awaiting helicopters. Redwine Security Element 1 (five

OPPOSITE
The *Cherry 1* crew under Major Irl Franklin pose with their MC-130E. They had to thread the needle in leading the formation of helicopters into North Vietnam at low altitudes. They would then circle the battle space, dropping flares and battle simulators to confuse the North Vietnamese. (USAF)

Captain Meadows (left foreground) and some of the Blueboy assault group. They are carrying CAR-15 rifles with 30-round magazines and the Singlepoint sights, acquired specifically for the raid, having greatly improved shooting accuracy during training. Meadows wears a red filter in his goggles to preserve his night vision against the blinding flares to be dropped during the raid. (USAF)

OPERATION *KINGPIN*

1 *Apple 3* destroys NW and SW guard towers to start raid.

2 *Banana* crash lands in courtyard on purpose and disgorges Dick Meadows and Blueboy team.

HQ Element and Meadows broadcast messages and secure courtyard.

Air Force Element (AF-*Banana* crew from crashed helo) and HQ Element (HQ) move to secure SW wall and blow a hole to move freed POWs through.

Action Element 1 (AE1) rescues and clears POWS cells 5A, 5C, 5D and NW corner.

Action Element 2 (AE2) clears building 5E and secures SE corner.

Action Element 3 (AE3) clears building 5B, secures east gate and links up with Greenleaf team on the outside.

3 *Apple 2* lands on the south side and disgorges Redwine team. As Plan Green is in effect with Greenleaf team engaged at the Secondary School, the Redwine mission changes.

Ground Force Command Post (CP) is set up at LZ and linked up with SW corner. Redwine Commander moves to assist with clearing east side.

Element 1 (E1) clears and secures buildings 8D, 4A, 8E and south wall, and links up with Blueboy holding SW corner and blown wall.

Element 2 (E2) moves to clear pumphouse to the south but reverses, clears, and secures east wall and east side 7B, 8B, 8F, and 8C buildings.

Element 3 (E3) is moved to the road and establishes blocking positions including a canal bridge.

The Pathfinder Element (PE) resumes clearing the pumphouse and then clearing telephone and concrete-power pole obstacles from the LZ.

road to
Song Cong
river bridge

13A
13B
DE
13C
GSG

bamboo gate
8A
7A
8B
8C
gardens
E2
SE
fish pond
7B
trench

Apple 1

GREENLEAF TEAM
GSG

to canal bridge

4 Once Bull Simons and the Greenleaf team are picked up from the Secondary School by *Apple 1*, they land outside the compound and resume their original mission.

Greenleaf Support Group (GSG) moves to secure the eastern side and support the demolition of the bridge to the north over the Song Cong River.

Demolition Element (DE) moves to destroy the bridge over the Song Cong River but Skyraiders are sent to destroy it. DE is then tasked to help secure the LZ.

Security Element (SE) moves to clear the area to the east and along the north to south road and buildings 13 A-C.

At the training site on Eglin AFB, Air Force liaison officer Major Keith Grimes and LTC Elliott Sydnor, Ground Force Commander with Redwine, discuss another night exercise. Grimes played a key role working weather planning into the operation which needed to be precise given the distances, variety of aircraft, and conditions they were flying into, especially with Typhoon Patsy on the way. (USAF)

Redwine Security Element 2 tasked with clearing the irrigation canal pumphouse and the area between the south wall and canal. Besides being fully loaded with ammunition, they carry M72 LAWs slung over their shoulders. (USAF)

men) would secure the terrain between the south wall and building 8D and to the west to the Song Con River. Element 2 (three men) would clear the pumphouse by the river and protect the approaches to the camp from enemy forces coming from the south. Element 3 (three men) would establish a defensive position near the small bridge and block enemy forces from approaching from the north, the Pathfinder Element (two men), would prepare the landing zone (LZ) for the helicopter by knocking down telephone poles, clearing hazards, and marking the LZs.

Greenleaf Support Group would arrive on HH-53 call sign *Apple 1*. Greenleaf would have three elements – a support element (six men), a demolition element (eight men), and a security element (five men) – plus the Alternate Ground Command of Bull Simons and his two radio operators. The support element would clear all the buildings east of the compound wall and north of the air raid shelter. The demolition element would move along the east compound wall, then destroy the bridge. The security element would cover the demolition team while it destroyed the bridge and cleared buildings east of the road.

The Greenleaf Support Group would sweep through the area housing communication facilities and enemy support troops and guards. It would secure the bridge north of the objective, cut communications cables, and blow up the bridge span closest to the objective. Raiders would sweep buildings across the road from the objective. They would have four 30lb satchel charges to drop on the bridge span and adhesive charges for cutting the cable.

The Greenleaf command group would establish blocking positions on the road south, the canal to the southwest, and the southwest corner of the compound wall.

Raiders would secure the freed POWs – disoriented, and confused or even overly excited – with lanyards attached to each other's wrists to ensure orderly movement and an accurate headcount. Raiders would move POWs to the southwest corner of the compound wall where they would be exfiltrated. Pilots would be ready to airlift up to 100 freed POWs.

In case there were unforeseen problems during the mission, there were alternate plans. Plan Blue assumed the Blueboy elements were unable to proceed. Redwine and Greenleaf would conduct the raid without Blueboy, with Redwine attacking the camp by going over and through the walls while Greenleaf forces conducted their original mission plus the original Redwine mission.

Plan Green assumed *Apple 1* and Greenleaf were gone. Redwine would have to fulfill the original Greenleaf mission and provide their own defense.

Plan Red assumed Redwine had failed. Greenleaf would split up and clear the buildings and guardhouses outside of the walls and provide their own defense.

All told, the final plan called for 56 ground troops and three crewmen of *Banana* to be fighting on the ground. Fifty-seven Air Force aircraft would get the men there and support them. Another 56 Navy aircraft would conduct diversionary raids and support missions. Confident of success, two men would act as photographers. The might of the US military was about to descend on North Vietnam if the weather cooperated.

The Tonkin Gulf Yacht Club Joins the Mission

Blackburn first proposed a US Navy diversionary mission at the first JCS meeting on July 10, 1970. While President Johnson had instituted a bombing campaign halt on March 31, 1968, the Navy still maintained a formidable presence on station in the Gulf of Tonkin, affectionately called "The Tonkin Gulf Yacht Club." Admiral Zumwalt deferred the idea to Vice Admiral Frederick A. Bardshar, commander of Task Force 77 (TF-77) in the Gulf of Tonkin.

Admiral John S. McCain, Commander in Chief of the US Pacific Command, received his first briefing on September 25 and was enthusiastic about the plan. McCain, of course, had a personal interest in the mission and knew the horrors the POWs faced day-to-day, tortured, barely fed, and living in deplorable conditions. His own son, John S. McCain III, was a POW. The North Vietnamese had captured the younger McCain on October 26, 1968 when his A-4E Skyhawk was shot down over Hanoi. During the bailout, he had fractured both arms and a leg, before landing in Truc Bach Lake where they fished him out and transferred him to Hoa Lo Prison, the infamous, "Hanoi Hilton."

In the ensuing months, the NVA tortured the younger McCain and only briefly relented when they found out his father was an Admiral. When the Hanoi government offered to release McCain to score propaganda points, McCain refused release unless Hanoi released every other prisoner captured before him. Hanoi did not take this refusal lightly and tortured him mercilessly.

On November 2, Admiral McCain met with Generals Blackburn and Manor for an update on the mission status as the forces prepared to deploy to Takhli RTAFB. Blackburn and Manor were to coordinate with Vice Admiral Bardshar but leave out Bardshar's superior, Vice Admiral Maurice F. Weisner at Seventh Fleet HQ in Yokosuka, Japan. Manor and Colonel Simons flew to the carrier USS *America* (CVA-66) to meet with Admiral Bardshar on November 5. On the Admiral's flagship, they briefed Bardshar, his Chief of Staff, and TF-77's intelligence officer on the rescue mission. They had a simple request:

Just prior to the appearance of the force from the west, diversionary penetrations by Navy air, consisting of two staggered thrusts toward the coast by squadron-sized forces beginning at H-20 minutes, are expected to trigger conventional air attack response by the North Vietnamese. The real effort will then be competing for resources and attention.

Bardshar immediately agreed to help, even volunteering forces to hit near Son Tay. Manor declined, saying he had that well under control.

However, the raid was taking place during the scheduled rotation of the TF-77 aircraft carriers. The *America* (CV-66) was scheduled to head back to the US on November 8 and the *Oriskany* (CVA-34) was due to leave during the time frame of the mission. The carriers USS *Hancock* (CVA-19) and *Ranger* (CV-61) would not arrive until after the mission. And the *Kitty Hawk* (CV-63) would not arrive until December. [9] Bardshar decided to extend the *Oriskany*'s stay in the Gulf of Tonkin until November 29, while bringing *Hancock* and *Ranger* into theater earlier, all the while keeping Seventh Fleet command out of the loop.

The Yacht Club prepared for the mission in absolute secrecy, with mission orders passed along only verbally to the carriers and escort ships. Secrecy was so strict that "Once this plan has been opened, no personal mail will leave your unit and personnel will be transferred only in emergency cases." Officers were only permitted to know "A special operation will be conducted by a Joint Contingency Task Group soon. It will be supported by elements of the TF-77 whose function is to create a diversion to assist in the successful execution of the basic mission."

The *Ranger*, *Oriskany*, and *Hancock* would launch a bewildering array of aircraft for the mission including fighter-bombers, tankers, SAR aircraft, and MIG CAPs. The first wave, or Track Alpha, would consist of four sections of A-7 Corsairs heading in at 8,000ft, 9,000ft, 10,000ft, and 11,000ft, respectively. The lead section would drop flares at H minus 4 minutes. The varying altitudes and flares would completely throw off the enemy. Track Bravo would consist of three sections of A7 aircraft flying at 17,000ft, 18,000ft, and 19,000ft. They would drop their flares at H minus 8 minutes. Finally, Track Charlie would see eight A6 Intruders heading in at 4,000ft over Haiphong Harbor dropping chaff. In total the strike packages and support aircraft would see at least 67 aircraft take off

A World War II veteran, the USS *Hancock*, along with the USS *Ranger*, and USS *Oriskany*, launched 58 aircraft in diversionary raids in support of the raid including fighters, bombers, tankers, early warning aircraft, and electronic jamming aircraft. The day after the raid, the USS *Hancock*, again launched attacks into North Vietnam as part of Operation *Freedom Bait*. (US Navy)

9   Gargus, June 2022

Air Actions and Flight Plans Approaching Son Tay

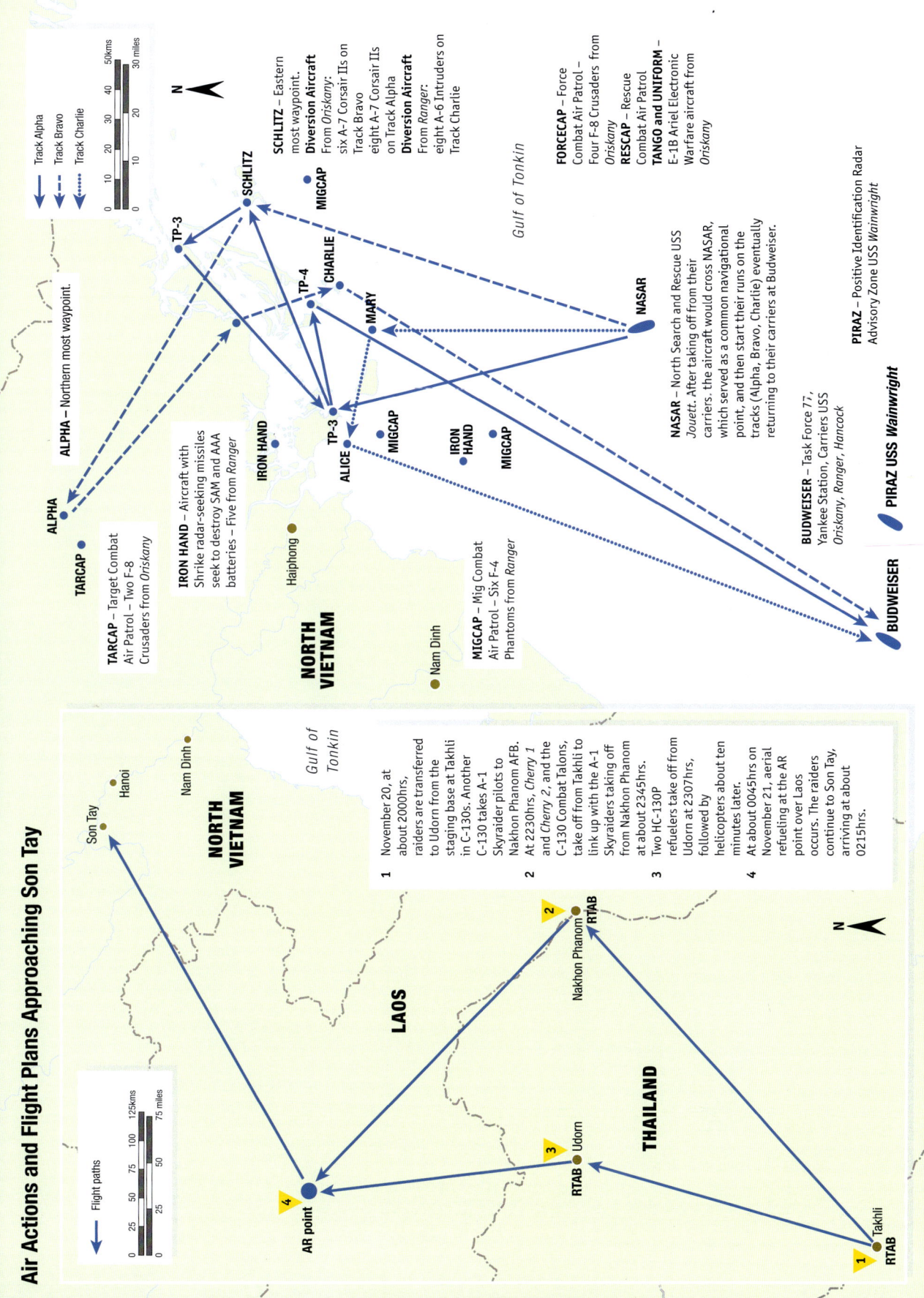

ALPHA – Northern most waypoint.

TARCAP – Target Combat Air Patrol – Two F-8 Crusaders from *Oriskany*

IRON HAND – Aircraft with Shrike radar-seeking missiles seek to destroy SAM and AAA batteries – Five from *Ranger*

MIGCAP – Mig Combat Air Patrol – Six F-4 Phantoms from *Ranger*

SCHLITZ – Eastern most waypoint.

Diversion Aircraft
From *Oriskany*:
six A-7 Corsair IIs on Track Bravo
eight A-7 Corsair IIs on Track Alpha

Diversion Aircraft
From *Ranger*:
eight A-6 Intruders on Track Charlie

Gulf of Tonkin

FORCECAP – Force Combat Air Patrol – Four F-8 Crusaders from *Oriskany*

RESCAP – Rescue Combat Air Patrol

TANGO and UNIFORM – E-1B Ariel Electronic Warfare aircraft from *Oriskany*

NASAR – North Search and Rescue USS *Jouett*. After taking off from their carriers. the aircraft would cross NASAR, which served as a common navigational point, and then start their runs on the tracks (Alpha, Bravo, Charlie) eventually returning to their carriers at Budweiser.

BUDWEISER – Task Force 77, Yankee Station, Carriers USS *Oriskany, Ranger, Hancock*

PIRAZ – Positive Identification Radar Advisory Zone USS *Wainwright*

Track Alpha
Track Bravo
Track Charlie

0 10 20 30 40 50kms
0 10 20 30 miles

NORTH VIETNAM

Haiphong

Nam Dinh

TP-3
SCHLITZ
MIGCAP
TP-4
CHARLIE
MARY
ALICE
TP-3
MIGCAP
IRON HAND
MIGCAP
NASAR
PIRAZ USS *Wainwright*
BUDWEISER
IRON HAND
ALPHA
TARCAP

N

Gulf of Tonkin

NORTH VIETNAM

Son Tay
Hanoi
Nam Dinh

LAOS

THAILAND

AR point
Udorn RTAB
Nakhon Phanom RTAB
Takhli RTAB

1. November 20, at about 2000hrs, raiders are transferred to Udorn from the staging base at Takhli in C-130s. Another C-130 takes A-1 Skyraider pilots to Nakhon Phanom AFB.

2. At 2230hrs, *Cherry 1* and *Cherry 2*, and the C-130 Combat Talons, take off from Takhli to link up with the A-1 Skyraiders taking off from Nakhon Phanom at about 2345hrs.

3. Two HC-130P refuelers take off from Udorn at 2307hrs, followed by helicopters about ten minutes later.

4. At about 0045hrs on November 21, aerial refueling at the AR point over Laos occurs. The raiders continue to Son Tay, arriving at about 0215hrs.

Flight paths

0 25 50 75 100 125kms
0 25 50 75 miles

N

from the three carriers. This would be the largest concentration of US naval aircraft since the start of the war, all for just a diversionary attack. The orders read, "the objective is to create as much confusion in the North Vietnamese Command and Control System as possible."

Rules of engagement did allow for defense. "Any aircraft over North Vietnam or the Gulf of Tonkin attacking or acting in a manner to attack friendly forces will be engaged." Because of the proximity of the friendly rescue support aircraft, any aircraft with a non-functioning Identification Friend or Foe (IFF) would be grounded. Aircraft were not authorized to pursue hostiles into territorial seas or airspace of China.

Last-Minute Intelligence Puzzles Everyone

In the last days before the raid, new intelligence was coming in about the camp. One bit from a North Vietnamese source, smuggled out in a cigarette packet, listed all known POW camps, but conspicuously absent was Son Tay. Did this mean the camp was empty, did the source have an incomplete list, was the camp unofficial or secret because of a high-value POW?

There was a brief discussion of moving the raid to nearby Dong Hoi, or Camp Faith, 15 miles closer to Hanoi. Planners dismissed the idea quickly. The information was too scant to guarantee reliability and all preparation, training, and rehearsals had gone into a raid targeting Son Tay. Besides, there was no way to tell if this information was any more or less accurate than other intelligence planners had.

Another highly classified clandestine mission was also looking at Son Tay as men and equipment arrived in Thailand for the raid. A small team of three Special Forces soldiers, two Vietnamese Kit Carson scouts and one CIA operative were inserted several miles from Son Tay and continued onward on foot. Their monitoring of Son Tay was as inconclusive as other bits of intelligence that fall. Under the lead of Sergeant Dale Dehnke, the team verified most of the information the SR-71 and drone flights had revealed, but, due to the height of the compound walls, they could not confirm the presence of POWs, nor did they see any outside the camp in work details. Once again, something seemed off about the intelligence concerning Son Tay.

The team managed to get close enough to also study the "Secondary School" and found enemy soldiers, capable of reaching the POW camp quickly just 500yds away. Another concern was that the site looked like a POW camp. In the confusion of a night raid, the helicopters could land there accidentally. A slight navigational error could put the helicopters landing next to the Secondary School.

Waiting in Thailand to Launch

On November 18, the rescuers landed at the RTAFB at Takhli, Thailand, to be greeted by General Manor

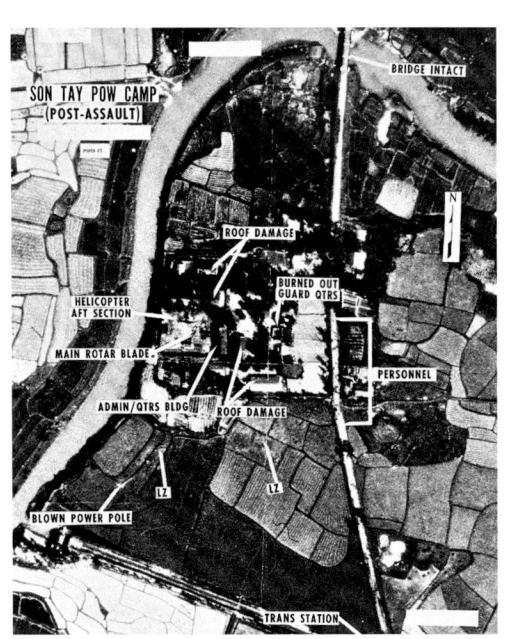

A post-raid reconnaissance photo shows the audacity, ferocity, and scope of the raid, with the Secondary School, just out of view in the South. For a brief period, American forces dominated a sizeable piece of territory in North Vietnam. The photo shows the remains of *Banana 1,* the burned out or damaged buildings inflicted by the HH-53 gunships or men on the ground, and the power pole downed to improve the LZ, and the contested bridges. (DOD)

and Colonel Simons. Manor had personally flown to Scott AFB, Illinois, to tell General P.K. Carlton, Commander in Chief of the Military Airlift Command, to release the necessary aircraft to fly the Son Tay raiders to Southeast Asia.[10] Besides the rescuers, the base also saw a noticeable uptick in civilians, who were actually Air Force doctors and nurses brought in to help with any sick and wounded from the mission. Despite the exhaustion and misery of jet lag, Simons gave them six hours of sleep. Simons and Manor later briefed them on their schedule and general mission parameters but still did not tell them exactly what the objective was. Obviously, they were somewhere in Southeast Asia and the target was war related. After going through the assault plans, they received dinner and a movie.

The Air Force crews arrived in Thailand, changed into their khaki uniforms to blend in better with the rest of the base personnel, and spent their last hours before the mission going over the flight routes, weather, and last-minute intelligence in a secure room. According to the intelligence officers, activity was visible in Son Tay, meaning the POWs were there.

Weighing on Manor and Simons' minds was Typhoon Patsy, on track to hit North Vietnam on November 21, the planned launch date. Could

10 Tilford, 107

A reconnaissance photo of the Son Tay POW camp, on the bottom right, clearly shows how the adjacent Son Cong River could easily flood the camp area during heavy rains. Flooding of the camp was theorized to be one of the reasons POWs were no longer kept there at the time of the raid. (Getty)

Just two days after the raid, on November 23, 1970, a tense press conference is held by, left to right, Secretary of Defence Melvin Laird, Colonel Arthur "Bull" Simons, Chairman of the Joint Chiefs of Staff Admiral Thomas Moorer, and Joint Contingency Task Group Brigadier General Leroy Manor. (Getty)

the mission launch earlier? Good weather and moonlight were critical for navigation and the safety of the aircraft. Turbulence would endanger the helicopters attempting to refuel. Low cloud coverage would disrupt any close air support from the A-1 Skyraiders tasked to cover the raiders. At sea, the US Navy forces conducting the diversionary mission needed good weather to launch, successfully drop their flares, then make it back to the carriers safely. Manor needed to know if the weather was going to permit the mission. Crosswinds were already approaching 30 knots in Da Nang, and extensive clouds and high winds were working their way into the Red River Delta. With winds expecting to pick up as the night wore on, the pilots added an extra five degrees north on their headings into camp. If they were not pushed off course, they would land at Son Tay further north, instead of south on top of the mysterious Secondary School.

Manor needed more weather intelligence which the Commander of the First Air Weather Service refused to hand over. To get that information, Manor had to go to the next higher headquarters, the Military Airlift Command's Air Weather Service at Scott AFB in Illinois. Manor, furious at the stupidity of it all, called Washington. The intransigent officer soon received a call from the Vice Commander of the Seventh Air Force that his career was about to go down in flames if he did not assist Manor.

Finally, after jerry-rigging a system of communications and generic wording to discuss weather among the different elements with incompatible equipment, complemented by two T-39s flying weather reports between Saigon and Takhli, Manor had a clear picture of the weather for the next few days. Over North Vietnam, a high-pressure ridge was just entering the area and might just clear Typhoon Patsy. Manor had a crucial decision to make – go on November 20 or wait seven days? Manor ordered a special weather reconnaissance and a meteorologist, transmitting, "Kingpin Six Urgently need expert weather forecaster ASAP. Can you provide?" A special weather reconnaissance flight of an RF-4 landed at Takhli with favorable data. Manor was relieved. The weather was going to be clear for at least 24 hours. Manor received his high-priority Red Rocket message and transmitted, "Kingpin Six Repeat Kingpin Six acknowledges receipt of Red Rocket One." He made his decision, moving Operation *Kingpin* up by one day. Manor gave the command and departed for his command post at Monkey Mountain, a signals intelligence base on Son Tra mountain, 20 miles east of Da Nang.

We Are Going to Rescue American Prisoners

Early on November 19, Simons woke the men for another walk-through. The Air Force search and rescue commander gave them briefings on SAR and their survival equipment and radio. Dick Meadows took the assault teams to re-zero their weapons after their shipment over and do a final cleaning. George Morton, the CIA operations chief from Udorn, gave another

After weeks of rigorous training in the in the sparse, hot, and humid Florida landscape under Colonel Simons, the men are prepared for a deep strike inside North Vietnam, but even at this point, they do not know their exact location or target. Carrying an array of weapons including M16s, CAR15s, M60s, M79s, LAWs, and all manors of explosives, the men are confident in success in whatever lies ahead. The uniform appearance includes Nomex fire retardant gloves and goggles to protect against the debris kicked up by helicopters. Some wear red-tinted lenses in the goggles to preserve their night vision as large diversionary flares are set off around the battlespace. (USAF)

escape and evasion briefing about rescue from Laos and more code signals. The men knew they were getting closer and closer to launching a mission.

On November 20, after breakfast, night vision equipment was issued, and Doc Cataldo issued sleeping pills and told the men to get some sleep. While they slept, Manor issued the final "Go" order. At 1700hrs, the men woke for a big meal. The majority still did not know what the mission was, and anticipation was reaching breaking point. At 1800hrs, Bull Simons finally broke the news.

> "We are going to rescue 70 Americans from a camp called Son Tay," Simons spoke to the assembled men. "This is something American prisoners have a right to expect." As many SAR missions had shown during the war, this was true, no matter where. After describing the location, he emphasized the POWs were the priority, "Our mission is to rescue prisoners, not take prisoners." Acknowledging they were going to be landing deep inside North Vietnam, on the outskirts of Hanoi, he let them know of the dangers if something went wrong. "Do not dream about walking out of North Vietnam." If things went wrong, Simons would keep them together and give the North Vietnamese a fight and make a last stand with their backs against the Son Cong River. "By Christ, let them come across that open ground. We will make them pay for every foot!"[11]

Simons looked out at them. Silence as they absorbed the news. And then the raiders stood up and applauded. Simons knew they were ready to go and enthusiastic about the mission. But not everybody was going. Simons had a number of standbys in case of injuries, dismissal for violations, or, at this point, if any of the primary candidates opted out. None did. The standbys would remain behind.

Now the men geared up for the long night ahead. Simons told Major Jay Strayer copilot of *Apple 2*: "If your flyboys don't pull us out, not to worry, we'll walk out without you!"[12] Strayer said he believed that if anyone could pull off such a feat, Simons could. One raider, typical of the rest of the force, carried a Colt M1911 .45-caliber pistol, a CAR-15 with eight 20-round magazines and five 30-round magazines, two fragmentation grenades, ten concussion grenades, a bulky PRC-25 radio, and a PRC-90 survival radio, knife, canteens, small rations, first aid kit, head-worn flashlight, and goggles. Spread among the men for specialized tasks were machetes, chain saws, wire cutters, bolt cutters, acetylene torches, and crowbars, as well as claymores, M60 machine guns, M79 grenade launchers, and demolition charges.

High above them, the last SR-71 reconnaissance flight was taking place. A "package" of SR-71 flights was planned to take one last look between November 20 and November 21 with the photos to be interpreted in theater. The latter took place, but the film was not processed until too late.

A HH-53C Jolly Green Giant on a Combat Search and Rescue (CSAR) mission. These extremely risky missions evolved over the course of the war, but the danger never went away. Nor did the bravery of the rescue personnel willing to go into harm's way to rescue fellow Americans. The rescue of BAT-21 in 1972 cost the lives of eleven rescuers, five aircraft shot down, and two rescuers captured. (USAF)

11 Hoe, 119
12 Chinnery, 244

THE RAID

Operation *Kingpin* Launches

Springing into action, ground troops and aircrews moved from their staging areas to launch bases with theater airlifts. Three C-130Es moved to U-Tapao RTAFB and were placed on alert for use by the JCTG. F-105 Wild Weasel and F-4 MIG CAP flight leaders moved to Korat RTAFB and Udorn RTAFB early on November 20. Another C-130E moved the helicopter and HC-130P took crews from Takhli RTAFB to Udorn RTAFB and took the A-1 Skyraider crews to Nakhon Phanom RTAFB. Another C-130E airlifted the assault force from Takhli RTAFB to Udorn RTAFB. Ground crews and fellow pilots who sensed the danger of the mission, having been told to stand down for a couple of days before so all aircraft and personnel could get some rest, wished them good luck.

With crews and forces in place, all manner of aircraft began their takeoffs. On board *Cherry 1* C-130E, pilot Captain William Guenon was struggling to get all four engines started. Engine Number Three refused to start after multiple tries. Likely the humidity of Thailand was causing a stuck bleed-air valve or intermittent electrical short. *Cherry 1* had practiced flying with three engines during training, and the mission was not going to be called off because of one engine. Finally, after one last attempt, the engine roared into life. The crew did a rolling takeoff, not wasting time to stop for taxiing and clearances, completing the pre-flight checklist while in-flight. By midnight the HH-3 and HH-53 helicopters, HC-130Ps refueling tankers, A-1E Skyraiders, F-4 Phantom MIG CAPs, F-105G Wild Weasel SAM Suppression aircraft, a KC-135 radio relay aircraft, KC-135 tankers, EC-121T College Eye, and a RC-135M Combat *Apple* were in the air. Weather and maintenance issues affected some flight plans, forcing some adjustments to routing or use of backup aircraft, but the aviation component of the assault was proceeding according to plan.

The helicopters and aircraft flew into North Vietnam under a partial moon, at an altitude of only 1,000ft and flying in a narrow corridor only

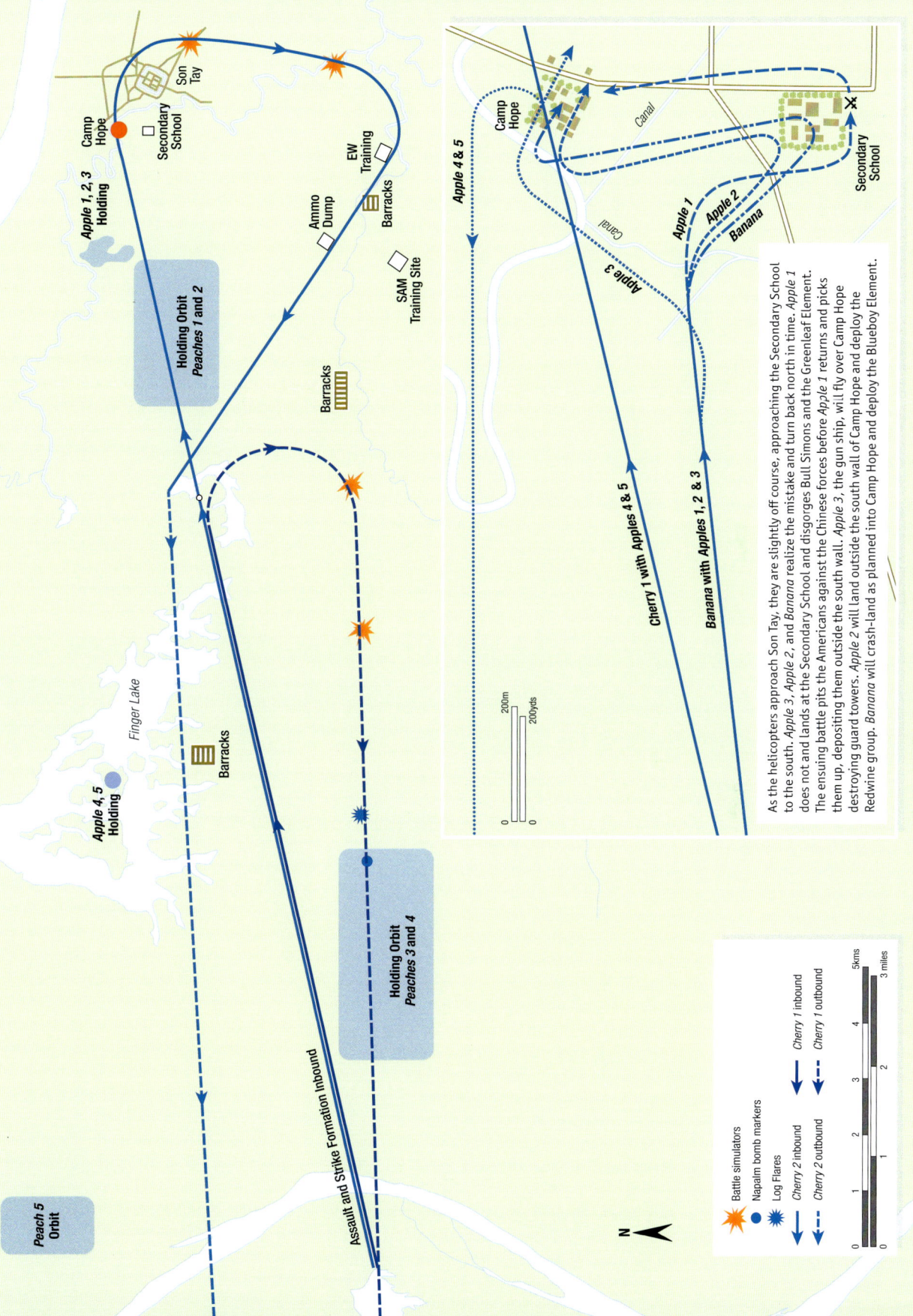

Apple 1, 2, 3
Holding

Son
Tay

Camp
Hope

Secondary
School

EW
Training

Ammo
Dump

Barracks

SAM
Training Site

Barracks

Holding Orbit
Peaches 1 and 2

Finger Lake

Barracks

Apple 4, 5
Holding

Holding Orbit
Peaches 3 and 4

Assault and Strike Formation Inbound

Peach 5
Orbit

N

Apple 4 & 5

Camp
Hope

Canal

Apple 1

Apple 2

Banana

Apple 3

Secondary
School

Canal

Cherry 1 with Apples 4 & 5

Banana with Apples 1, 2 & 3

200m

200yds

As the helicopters approach Son Tay, they are slightly off course, approaching the Secondary School to the south. *Apple 3*, *Apple 2*, and *Banana* realize the mistake and turn back north in time. *Apple 1* does not and lands at the Secondary School and disgorges Bull Simons and the Greenleaf Element. The ensuing battle pits the Americans against the Chinese forces before *Apple 1* returns and picks them up, depositing them outside the south wall. *Apple 3*, the gun ship, will fly over Camp Hope destroying guard towers. *Apple 2* will land outside the south wall of Camp Hope and deploy the Redwine group. *Banana* will crash-land as planned into Camp Hope and deploy the Blueboy Element.

Battle simulators

Napalm bomb markers

Log Flares

Cherry 2 inbound

Cherry 2 outbound

Cherry 1 inbound

Cherry 1 outbound

0 1 2 3 4 5kms

0 1 2 3 miles

Blueboy assault group in the final dress rehearsal under Captain Dick Meadows (bottom left). They have with them two items needed to pull off the raid – acetylene torches to cut through metal locks and chains holding the POWS and the large fire-fight simulator, essentially a white box of firecrackers designed to confuse the enemy as to the direction of the battle. (USAF)

6 miles wide, using the terrain to mask their approach. The low altitudes, slow speeds, and low visibility affected navigational systems and pilot bearings, but the FLIR was performing flawlessly. The aircraft descending on Son Tay were on time and on target, threading the hills, often barely clearing the trees.

Most of the men were experienced veterans and during the three-hour flight they sat in the helicopters mentally preparing for the danger ahead or getting some sleep. At one point the radio came alive with "break, break, break" meaning that one aircraft had lost sight of the formation. Per hours of practice and rehearsals, the helicopters turned to a predetermined heading and climbed to a predetermined altitude for one minute then returned to the original flight plan. An unknown aircraft had almost run into the formation and the break was called to avert a mid-air collision. The riskiest part of the flight was always the mid-air refueling and formation changes with one collision avoided by one crew waving off another by shining a flashlight at the cockpit.

As *Cherry 1* approached Son Tay, the pilot called out, "Alpha! Alpha! Alpha!" At 500ft, the plane turned southeast and dropped two battlefield simulators south and southeast of Son Tay. The still night erupted in what anyone would have assumed was a massive firefight. It then dropped a BLU-27/B firebomb marker, but one other misfired and was jettisoned in a lake west of the objective. The HK-6 log flares were stuck behind the misfired BLU-27/B at first so, after jettisoning the bad BLI-27/B, the crew decided not to drop the HK-6s out of sequence for fear of confusing friendly forces.

"Beautiful!" one of the pilots shouted over the radio. The diversion signaled the raid was on and, within seconds, someone called out, "Where are the tracers coming from?"

SAM radar activity was immediately detected, forcing the EC-130E to take evasive action and to duck behind the hills at less than 1,000ft, where it spent the rest of the mission, avoiding SAMs.

Civilians, accustomed to the bombing halt, thought it was a massive attack. One recalled,

That night, we had been sleeping for a while when we heard the roar of aircraft overhead and the sound of guns firing wildly all over the area. The electricity went out, but suddenly the skies lit up like it was daylight. Later I learned that the light was from American illumination flares. Because our school constantly reviewed our lessons on the need for vigilance, we guessed that something dangerous was happening.[13]

Apple 3, the HH-53 flown by Major Frederic M. Donohue, "Marty," with his copilot Captain Thomas R. Waldron, and his crew of Staff Sergeant

13 Hung, 53

Aaron P. Hodges, Staff Sergeant James J. Rogers, and Staff Sergeant Angus W. Sowell III, was rapidly approaching Son Tay at treetop level. They were barely 40ft above ground and searching for the crucial landmarks of the Song Con River with a small branch flowing to the west of the POW camp. The lights of Hanoi were visible in the distance.

Inside the helicopters, the assault teams braced themselves for the battle ahead. If anything went wrong, they could end up as POWs themselves. It would be an embarrassment of unprecedented scale for the United States. Even with the bravado of Bull Simons' speech just a brief time earlier, it was still a scary proposition. The mission had to succeed and, no matter what, they would pull it off. At H-5 minutes, the men stood up, secured their seats out of the way, removed tape from grenades, readied an M72 LAW, chambered rounds, and braced for assault.

Something was wrong though. Helicopters were finicky, and *Apple 3* was no exception. On its most important mission, *Apple 3*, without warning, developed a problem. Captain Waldron pointed to a yellow warning light flashing, "Transmission." Normally, a transmission light would mean landing the helicopter immediately. The pilot, Marty Donohue, weighed his options, either declare an emergency and land *Apple 3*, jeopardizing the mission, or push his luck. If the transmission failed, he could kill his entire crew. If he landed, and did not destroy the guard towers, many raiders could be killed. The stakes were high. "Ignore it!" *Apple 3* was going ahead, failing transmission or not.

At Eglin Air Force Base, the *Apple* crews pose in front of an HH-53. With countless hours of flight time and experience in Search and Rescue missions, they were the best crews for a deep strike into North Vietnam to rescue the POWs at Son Tay. (Thomas Waldron)

The *Apple 3* crew after receiving their medals at Fort Bragg. Pilot Major Frederic "Marty" Donohue, Copilot Captain Thomas Waldron, Staff Sergeant Aaron Hodges, Staff Sergeant James Rogers, and Staff Sergeant Angus Sowell III were tasked with obliterating the guard towers with the HH-53 miniguns firing out each crew door and the lowered rear ramp. Copilot Waldron recently said he can still see the blaze out his cockpit window in his head. (Thomas Waldron)

But now they were off course. In the alternating darkness and skies lit up by the diversionary flares from the C-130s – and the adjustment to the course earlier because of expected winds and the concern over the transmission – Marty did not notice they were 200yds south. If they were off course, they would miss hitting the guard towers before the other raiders approached, endangering the mission. Flares silhouetted the buildings, and it looked like they were right on target. Marty realized something was wrong when the guard towers did not come into view as expected. His copilot looked for a critical landmark – a small tributary west of the Son Tay camp coming from the Hong River. Waldron yelled, "That's not it! No river!" Waldron scanned the terrain, frantically looking for the river. To his left it appeared, "There it is!" he called out and pointed Marty in the right direction. Marty paused to regain his bearings, and made a steep turn to the left headed north.[14]

Behind him were Meadows' Blueboy team in *Banana*, Sydnor's Redwine in *Apple 2*, and Simons' group, Greenleaf, in *Apple 1*. Marty was about to break radio silence to warn everyone they were off course but did not, when, with great relief, *Apple 2* and *Banana* turned with him, heading north and back on target.

It was vitally important they hit the two guard towers and the barracks outside the east wall. *Apple 3* was now flying directly over the compound, with Marty quickly gaining altitude to clear the trees in the compound. The crew held on to the three miniguns tightly, they would get one shot at this and had to be ready no matter how much *Apple 3* jerked about. Marty dropped the HH-53 again past the trees in the courtyard and flared the helicopter.

"Fire!" Marty commanded.

The guards, distracted by the flares in the distance, likely never knew what hit them. Instantly the miniguns let loose hundreds of rounds. The 7.62mm rotary-barrel M134 miniguns could fire up to 6,000 rounds per minute and disintegrate any target they hit. Firing the guns mounted on either side of the crew hatches and on the rear ramp, the crews did not miss. An A-1E Skyraider pilot flying his hold pattern recalled, "the towers blew apart or caught fire, as did the guard quarters."[15]

The Assault on Son Tay

"We got 'em, we got 'em!" his gunners yelled over the intercom. *Apple 3* immediately headed north, then circled around the camp to a holding area to the west of the camp. The HH-53 set down and the crew took up defensive positions, with the engines running, rather than take a chance on a cold start. All the while, Waldron worried if the transmission would fail and they would need to hitch a ride home themselves.[16]

14 Waldron, 120
15 Isby
16 Waldron, 120

Banana, the HH-3 piloted by Lieutenant Colonel Herbert E. Zehnder and his crew of Major D. Kalen and Technical Sergeant Leroy M. Wright, was coming in fast and hard. Onboard were the 13 men of Dick Meadows' assault group. The ramp, window, and door gunners fired at their targets, tracer rounds lighting up their targets. *Banana*, flying at treetop level, "tore into one tree like a big lawn mower," Major Kalen later recounted. The blades were damaged, but *Banana* was coming in as planned. *Banana* slammed into the ground, inside the compound. The impact jostled the assault team, lying on mattresses to absorb the impact.

First Lieutenant George L. Petrie, thrown out of the HH-3 by the impact, was the first raider out of *Banana*. Meadows and the rest of his assault force scrambled out of the helicopter. Technical Sergeant Wright, fighting through the pain of a broken ankle from the crash, came out of the wreckage to continue with the mission. About 15yds from the mangled wreck of the helicopter, Meadows began calling through his bullhorn, "We are Americans! Keep your head down! This is a rescue! Get on the floor!" So far, so good, as the assault team headed to the cells. The guards, recovered from the shock of the assault, began to fire on the raiders.

Methodically, the raiders killed any enemy they encountered; they were not there to take prisoners.

Meadows' radio operator called Sydnor on the command net, "Wildroot, this is Blueboy. We are in." The raiders were hitting the cellblocks to get the American POWs out and take them home. Simons' group would be right behind them.

While Meadows was calling out to the prisoners, the Headquarters Element cleared building 3 and blew a 4ft x 4ft hole in the wall. The assault element moved to Cell Block 5A, splitting into two-man teams. After two men cleared a guard tower, they moved along the interior west and north wall

Facing east towards the "Cat House," the remains of *Banana 1* shows the daring skill of the pilot to crash land inside the compound with no room for error. The original idea of having the raiders fast-rope into the compound was rejected early in planning because it would leave the men and helicopters exposed to fire for too long. The smaller UH-1 Huey was considered for this tactic, but was rejected because it couldn't carry enough men. (USAF)

BANANA 1 CRASH LANDS IN THE MIDDLE OF SON TAY POW CAMP

0221hrs November 21, 1970, *Banana 1*, an HH-3, crewed by Pilot Major Herbert D. Kalen, Copilot Lieutenant Colonel Herbert R. Zehnder, and Technical Sergeant Leroy M. Wright intentionally crash lands in the middle of the Son Tay POW camp, disgorging the Blueboy Assault Group, led by Captain Richard J. Meadows. As the men fan out to assault the prison cells, Captain Meadows announces on a bullhorn several times, "We are Americans! This is a rescue!" The assault team, armed with primarily 5.56mm CAR-15 rifles, carrying acetylene torches and bolt cutters to cut through holding chains, clear the buildings decisively, helped in their precision shooting by Singlepoint red dot rifle sites and countless hours on the range and camp mockup back in Florida. The men are uniformly wearing the popular jungle fatigues, stripped of ranks and emblems, field caps, and goggles, both as protection from the debris kicked up by the landing and rotors shredding trees and to keep from being blinded by the diversionary flares. Within moments, North Vietnamese guards are dead, buildings are ablaze, but the POWs are nowhere to be found.

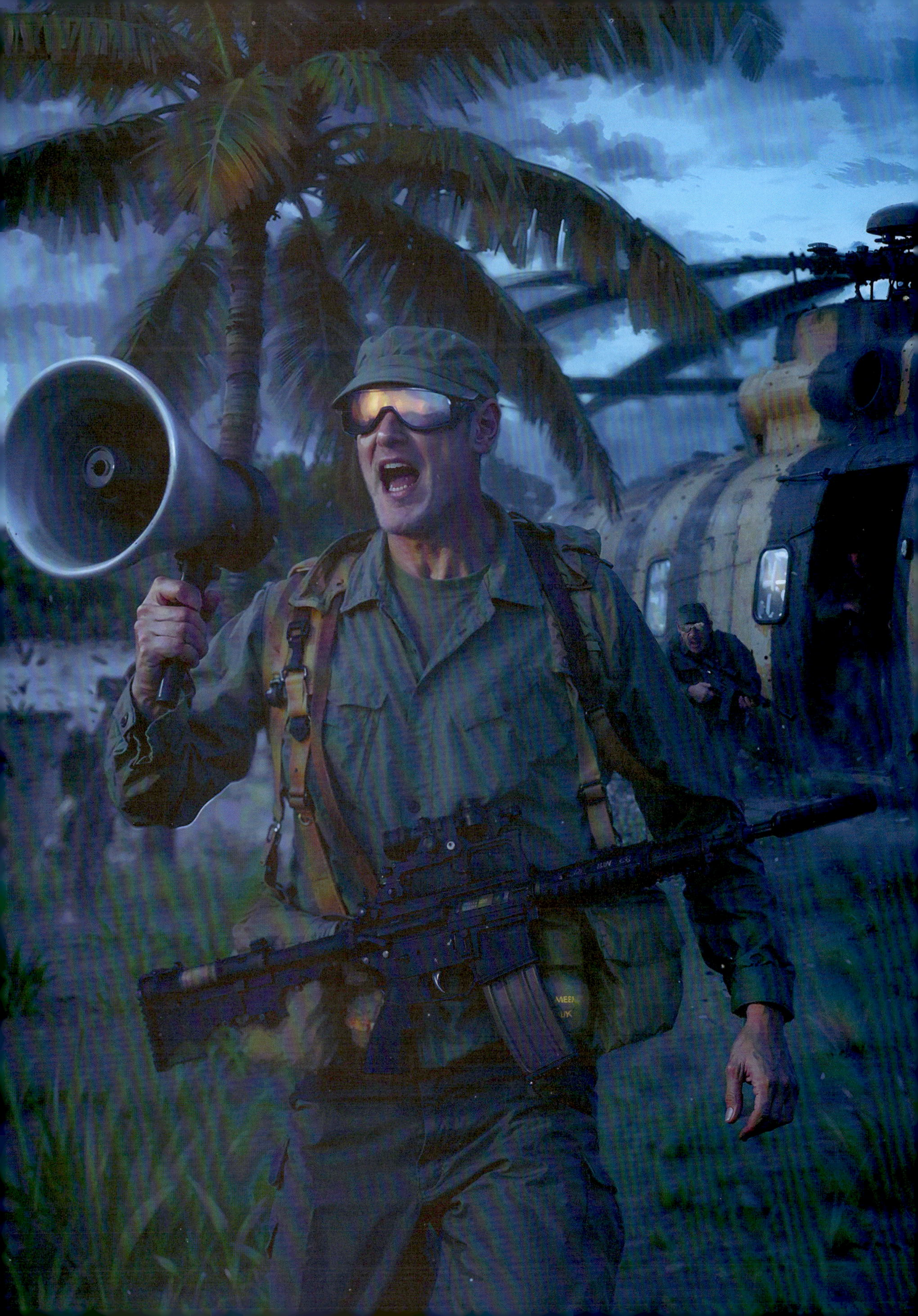

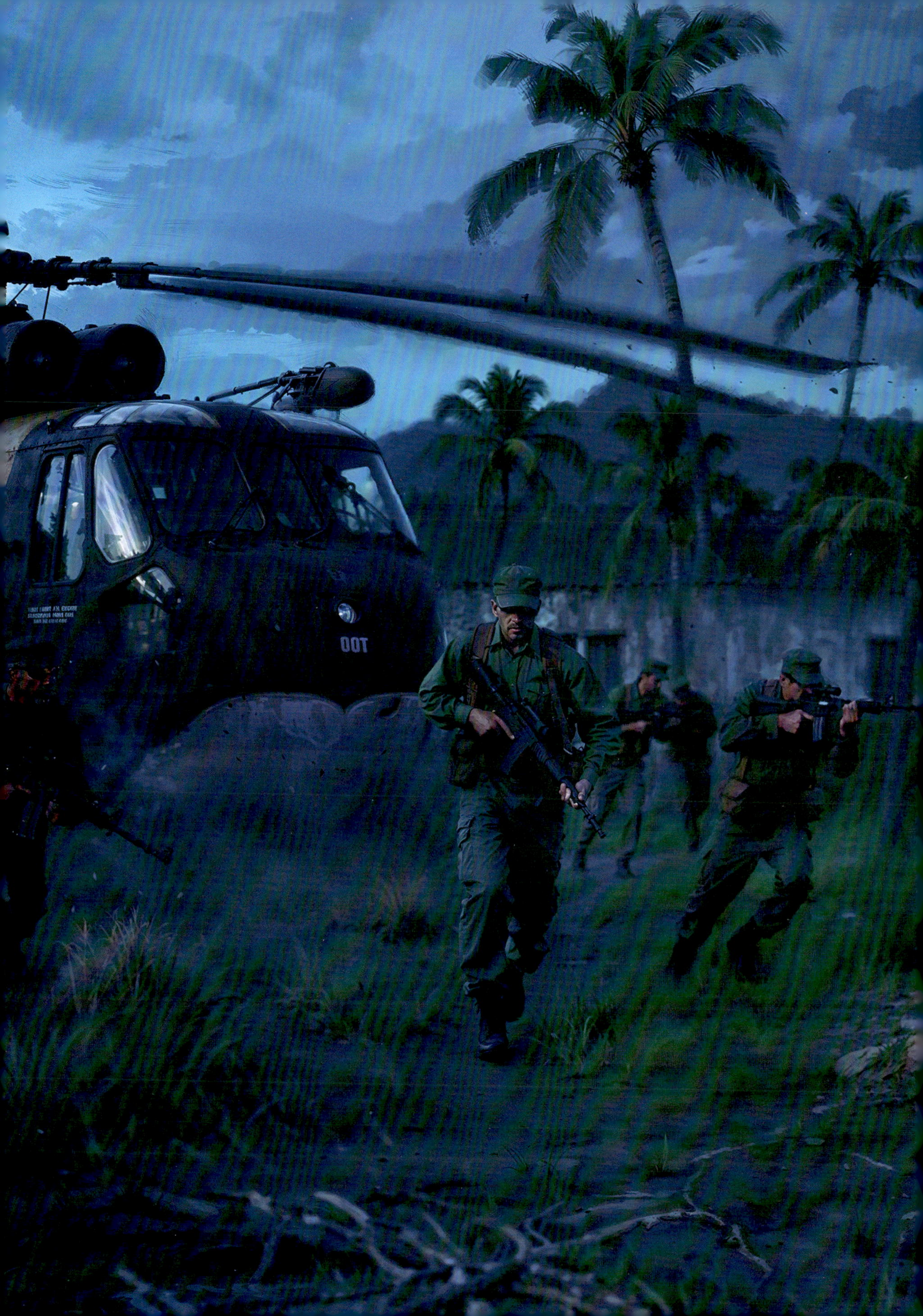

The wreckage of *Banana*, the HH-3 carrying Dick Meadows and the Blueboy assault team, rests in the courtyard of the Son Tay camp with its tail near the west wall. In an astounding act of bravery, *Banana* came in low and fast and intentionally crash landed inside the camp for maximum surprise. Only one soldier received a minor ankle injury in the landing. As the raid ended, *Banana* was destroyed in place, as planned, with C4 explosives. (USAF)

before entering Cell Block 5C. At Cell Block 5D another team of two men startled several guards who were killed trying to flee through the gate.

The raiders cleared Cell Block 5E and 4, killing more guards. The Blueboy elements were clearing the cell blocks with precision. The men did not have time to contemplate why two of the locked cells they cleared had more than 100lb of cement and metal bars but no prisoners.

Meadows' team was methodically going through the camp breaking into one prison cell after the other to free the prisoners from their 6 x 8 concrete cells. Building 5B had six cells with three entrances. A partition separated the hallway between every two cells. In the well-designed cells, even one determined guard could inflict serious casualties on the raiders.

Within eight to ten minutes, the cell blocks were clear with no casualties to report so far.

At the south wall, the Blueboy Headquarters Element was tasked with blowing a hole in the wall for Bull Simons' Greenleaf Element.

Except Simons was not where he was supposed to be. Sydnor, as *Apple 2* landed outside the POW camp walls, was afraid Simons' team had been shot down or forced down with mechanical problems. Either way, just over two minutes into the assault, the mission was down one helicopter and 22 men. Sydnor quickly put Plan Green into effect – the alternative plan in case of the loss of Simons' helicopter and designed to complete the mission with less men. Sydnor told *Apple 2* to open fire with their miniguns on guard building 7B reserved for Simons' *Apple 1* gunners.

On board Redwine's helicopter, *Apple 2*, the youngest Green Beret on the mission, Terry Buckler, steadied himself. This would be his first combat mission and the countless practice assaults didn't alleviate his fears. The door gunners opened fire on their targets and Redwine's helicopter landed. The Ground Force Commander, Lieutenant Colonel Elliott Sydnor and his security elements and pathfinders fanned out to begin their planned assaults and take on the missing Greenleaf team objectives. Buckler immediately spotted an enemy soldier, placed the Singlepoint sight dots on the soldier's chest and fired.[17] Sydnor's headquarters element then came under fire by building 7B which they just as quickly suppressed with an M79 40mm grenade launcher and an M60 machine gun.

Redwine Security Element 3 set off to the southwest to secure a small bridge over a canal about 200yds away to prevent enemy forces from reaching the camp. Claymores were set up in defensive positions to slow down any enemy approaching Son Tay while the assault and extraction were continued. Meanwhile, Doc Cataldo prepared to receive the first prisoners and wounded.

Redwine took more fire from the east side of the main road just 15yds away from North Vietnamese armed with ancient M1 carbines.

17 Buckler, 100

The team continued to clear buildings and kill guards as they found them, assaulting each building with precision, honed after weeks of training. There was a brief moment of levity as one building they cleared had only ducks.

One raider assaulted the pump station with a concussion grenade and then fired a full magazine of 30 rounds into it. He then joined the other Pathfinder in trying to knock down an electrical pole.

As Redwine prepared for extraction, they came under fire from building 8D. The assault on the building killed another seven NVA. Approaching the building, First Sergeant Joseph Murray took a fragmentation grenade, released the spoon, and was about to throw it into the window when he felt his leg "convulse forward and burn as the bullet hit me." He still managed to grab the windowsill and drop the grenade in. The three NVA targeting him to the rear were killed by Master Sergeant Herman Spencer. Brushing off his wound because "there was no time to stop" the two proceeded to clear the building.[18]

More NVA were engaged across the river with M79 grenade launchers and rifle fire. At the same time, a convoy of four or five trucks came into view about 200yds away heading their way. Redwine engaged them with an M72 LAW, halting them.

The raging battle shocked Son Tay civilians. Tran Thi Nghien, recalled,

I suddenly woke up because I heard the roar of a propeller-driven aircraft flying over my house. I looked through the corner of a window and saw many bright lights, and then there came the sound of gunfire, so loud it hurt my ears. I saw big, tall men wearing steel helmets. They were yelling things that I could not understand and running back and forth. My husband, Can Huu An, whispered in my ear, "They are not our troops conducting a practice exercise."[19]

18 Gargus, 210
19 Hung, 51

At Eglin AFB, Florida, one of the raiders, armed with a CAR-15, wearing the raid uniform of jungle fatigues, pauses during training in the middle of the now legendary cloth mockup of the Son Tay camp. A security analysis of the training determined any aerial recognition of the structures or target area was impossible. (USAF)

REDWINE SECURITY ELEMENT 3 SECURE A CANAL BRIDGE

0222hrs November 21, 1970, Redwine Security Element 3, consisting of Sergeant First Classes Donald D. Blackard, Gregory T. McGuire, and Freddie D. Doss race past guard quarters and buildings down the road to secure a canal bridge and prevent North Vietnamese forces south of the camp from counter-attacking. Knowing they would be on their own, covered only by A-1 Skyraiders circling overhead, they are heavily armed, each carrying Claymore mines and M72 66mm light anti-tank weapons. Additionally, Doss carries an M60 7.62mm machine gun, McGuire carries an M79 40mm grenade launcher, while Blackard carries his 5.56mm M16. The three, separated from the main force, race through the terrain eerily lit by flares, moonlight, and the fires from the raging battle behind them, not knowing how big of an attack they would face.

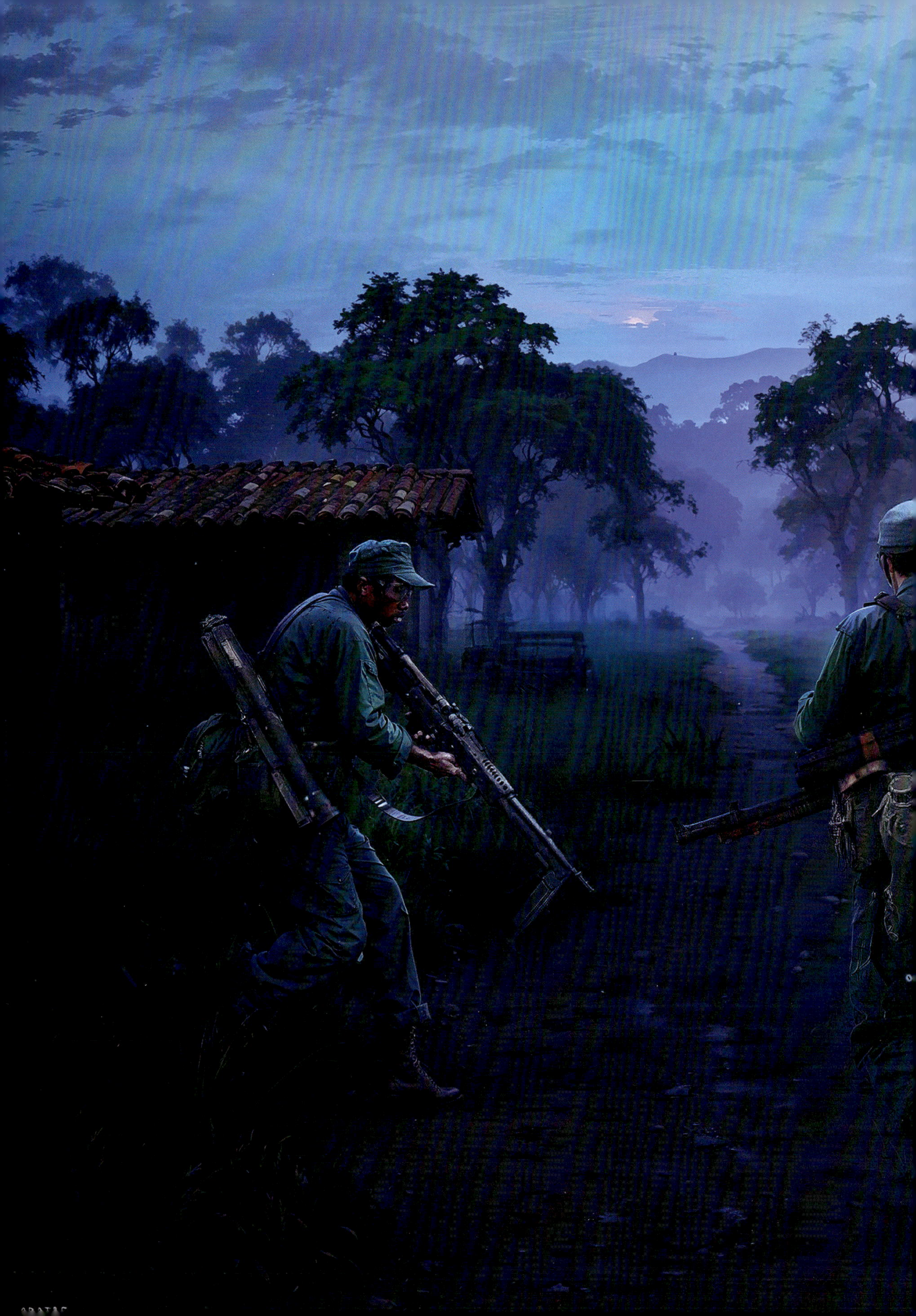

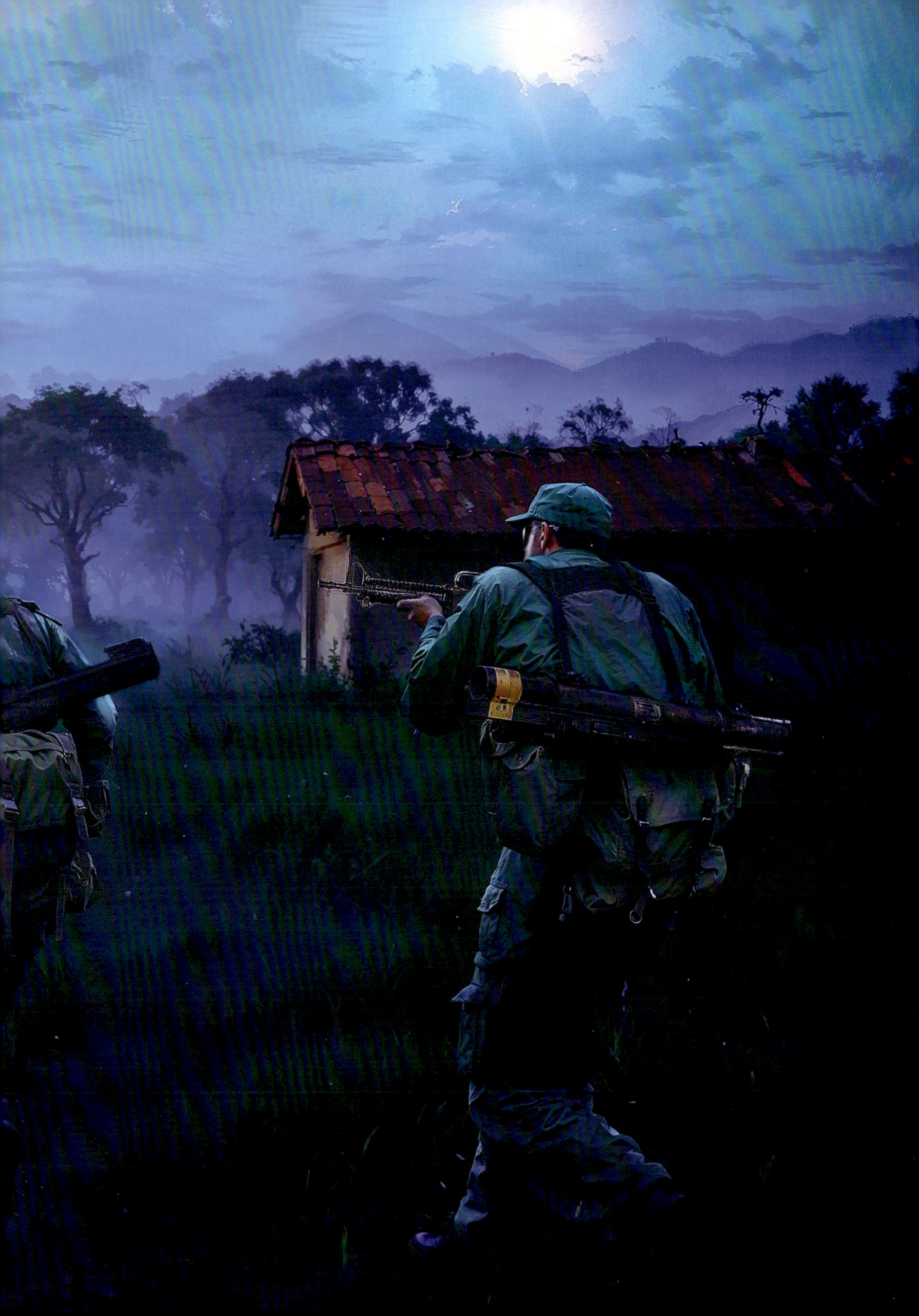

The Secondary School Battle

Instead of turning north with the other helicopters, *Apple 1*, piloted by Lieutenant Colonel Warren Britton, carrying Simons' team and Greenleaf troops, continued, and landed at the Secondary School compound. *Apple 2* called *Apple 1* after *Apple 1* lifted off, "Hey you set them down in the wrong place, friend! Did you leave them out?" Simons and his 22 men were moving into assault positions when Simons realized the error as they came under fire.

Apple 1 was already headed to the holding area, leaving Simons and his men exposed on the ground. Caught completely off guard, one enemy emerged from his fighting positions clad only in his underwear, with Simons recalling, "He was frightened, I mean really frightened, dumbfounded. We landed out of nowhere. I remember thinking, 'This is a lousy time of night for introductions.' I shot him through the chest."

"This is Axle, we're in the wrong place," Simons, using his code word, transmitted. *Apple 1* called back, "we'll come and get you."

In the heat of battle, radio transmissions were misunderstood and when someone called out "Axle," was "lost," the reaction in some was shock. "We've lost Axle! We lost Axle!" the Skyraider command and control kept yelling, "God damn, Simons has been killed, we're all in deep shit." It took a moment before the pilots realized Simons wasn't dead.[20]

Staff Sergeant Walter L. Miller, Simons' radio operator, tried to raise *Apple 1* with Simons yelling, "Get that fucking chopper back in here!" Unaware of Sydnor's actions, Simons also ordered Plan Green. Simons' signal team moved quickly to set up a strobe light and mark a landing zone.

Simons' group, under heavy fire, knew to attack. His men advanced into the Secondary School killing any fighters that emerged to engage them. The men ruthlessly cleared the southern billets with rifle and grenades, determined to neutralize the threat. From the western edge of the Secondary School, Greenleaf was receiving fire and an M60 machine gun eliminated this threat. From a two-story building in the center of the compound, automatic fire rained down on them. An M79 40mm grenade launcher placed accurate fire through the windows and doors to kill the enemy.

Who exactly they were firing at was unknown. The hostiles coming out engaging Simons' men were clearly not North Vietnamese. They were much taller, wearing t-shirts and dark undershorts and much better equipped than other guards at the perimeter and at the POW camp. The enemy Simons was ruthlessly killing were either Chinese or Russian personnel, possibly there to train North Vietnamese on air defense and warning systems.

As the raiders waited for the helicopter to get them, they killed several enemy attempting to reach a two-story building. As Britton and *Apple 1* approached, Simons conducted a fighting withdrawal toward the landing zone. *Apple 1* called, "Give us a flare, give us a flare and we'll come and get you." Simons masterfully reoriented his men from the attack to securing the LZ and conducting a fighting withdrawal, with Simons' headquarters

20 Waresh

element the last to board *Apple 1*. They had been on the ground for only six minutes but exacted a terrible toll on the enemy. *Apple 1* took off with all of Simons' men aboard, the Secondary School on fire, and many enemy forces of unknown origin dead. Simons finally reached Meadows and Sydnor telling them the "basic plan" was still on.

Negative Items, I Repeat, Negative Items!

Back at Son Tay, the assault group under Meadows still searched the camp and cleared the POW cells, as planned in case of Plan Green.

In less than a minute *Apple 1* disgorged Simons' team again, this time in the correct location. Simons' demolition team took off to blow up the bridge north of the camp and Sydnor's men continued with destroying the power stations, power lines, and pumphouse. Despite the initial separation, the raid was going as planned.

Except something was amiss. Meadows' and Snyder's forces had overwhelmed the guards, killing dozens. The only real resistance came from around a well inside the compound and a building just south of the compound's west wall. Throughout the compound dozens of the enemy were dead. Another two dozen guards were dead or wounded south of the compound. Simons' men killed another ten in the headquarters building outside the front gate and barracks next to it.

The mission was proving to be an overwhelming success if they could now get everyone out safely. But then one by one, the raiders called out, "Negative items." Meadows and the men could not believe it. The POWs had to be somewhere. The raiders searched every building. Meadows went to the cellblocks himself. They were empty. Dejected, he called over the command net, "Wildroot, this is Blueboy: Negative items. All the buildings have been searched. Negative items." A few seconds later he called again, as if not believing it himself, "Search complete: Negative items."

Simons did not let his disappointment show and accepted it as a fait accompli, "Blueboy, understand. Negative items. Standby to withdraw normally." With no time to contemplate what had gone wrong, Simons ordered, "Withdraw to the LZ. Blueboy and Redwine exit on the first extraction. Set up LZ security: Redwine to the west, Greenleaf to east. Normally, as planned."

Simons continued to coordinate the helicopters, "Redwine, negative items in the compound. Standby to make departure normally. Advise me when the LZ is marked and advise me when you have contact with all personnel." Greenleaf's security element called Simons, "What's the situation?" Simons replied, "There are negative items. Pull back to the east side of the LZ. We'll go out as normal." A few minutes later, "This is Greenleaf, we're off bubba."

A photographer raced through the compound taking photos of the empty cells, as if their eyes were deceiving them. Somebody called over the

One of the pilots examines the cloth mockup of the Son Tay POW camp in an isolated training area at Eglin AFB, Florida. The cloth mock up, deceptively simple, proved effective as an outline of the prison walls and buildings, giving the men ample opportunity to practice the raid without having to build a full camp. (USAF)

On April 27, 1973, H. Ross Perot, Texas millionaire businessman and long-time advocate for POWs, sponsored a parade and celebration of the Son Tay raiders and former POWs in San Francisco. At the Fairmont Hotel, now-retired Colonel "Bull" Simons sits with former POWs Navy Commander Render Clayton and Air Force Colonel James Risner. (National Archives)

radio, "Do you have items, Blueboy?" Again, Meadows transmitted, "Negative."

Simons called, "Move to our location. Your entire element. If there are negative items, continue to normal LZ." *Apple 1* called out to Meadows, "Blueboy we have first packet ready for delivery. Do you have items currently?" Meadows, again responded, "Negative."

"*Apple 1*, there are negative items, come in your normal LZ," Simons directed. Wildroot ordered Blueboy too, "Take your entire element out on *Apple 1*. Pass through me."

Greenleaf wanted to know which helicopter was for his element, "Possibly *Apple 2* or *3*." The mission's success now rested on getting the raiders out intact. The missing prisoners could not distract them. The ground controller fired off a flare to guide *Apple 1* into the LZ.

To clear the LZ, they had to cut down light poles with a chainsaw. But they encountered a concrete pole. This required C-4 to blow it. Except it was not a light pole, but four large high-tension powerlines. The lines came down in the rice paddies meant to be an LZ. A quick assessment by the Marshalling Area Control Officer got their LZ moved a little further away to avoid electrocution.

The Air Battle

Overhead, two A-1 Skyraiders in an orbit of 3,000ft heard the call from the Ground Force Commander to attack the footbridge to the southwest and any road targets, "We'll take care of the big bridge. I say again, the big bridge now." The A-1s dropped four white-phosphorus 100lb bombs on the target and then conducted two strafing runs. Some of the bombs fell short, taking out a number of buildings between the camp and the built-up area known as the "Citadel."[21] SAMs then began appearing.

Calls of "SAM, SAM, SAM!" came over the radio continuously.

After three more strafing runs, command told the pilots the rescue team was pulling out. The A-1s jettisoned their remaining ordinance in Black River before resuming orbit and flying back. An A-1 Skyraider obliged a close air support request with a strafing run on the bridge with its 20mm cannon to stop suspected reinforcements from arriving.

After dropping its firebomb markers and log flares on target, the C-130E began orbiting the battlefield. Thirteen minutes into the mission, the aircraft picked up SAM radar activity and the pilot took evasive action, dropping to low-altitude maneuvers behind hills, at less than 1,000ft altitude. Another crew called out, "Stay down nice and low. No sweat." The crew knew they had made the right decision as they spotted SAMs heading toward targets.

21 Waresh

The NVA 361st Air Defense Division ordered a Condition One alert around 0218hrs as it picked up inbound aircraft but was confused about where aircraft were coming from.[22]

The A-1 pilots also spotted the SAMs as they made their strafing runs. To gain speed as soon as they finished their strafing runs, the three A-1s dropped their remaining ordnance and departed the area. Another A-1 pilot remained in orbit west of Son Tay with lights on to draw away MIGs from the ground battle.

The F-4D MIG CAP aircraft stayed in an orbit of 16,000–18,000ft, searching for any inbound MIGs. Their radar warning instruments picked up AAA and SAM radars and the crews performed evasive maneuvers. Fortunately, the equipment worked as intended, perfected after years of war, and the pilots picked up the SAMs or saw the orange fireball of a launch and white-orange flame from the missiles as they ascended. The SAMs kept coming though. "SAM! SAM! SAM!" The pilots continued to shake off the missiles, talking to each other and utilizing every tactic they had, including low-level calling out, "drop lower. Stay down low. Nice and low. No sweat. Stay down. Lower yet. Go on down. Lower yet. Down on the deck. I'll tell you where it is. It's on your tail. Turn left!"

POWs kept at Dong Hoi, "Camp Faith," 15 miles to the east heard the battles in the distance and the launching of SAMs. They knew a rescue effort was underway, just in the wrong place, but it still boosted their morale. Orson Swindle recalled hearing "all hell breaking loose" in the direction of their camp and realizing a raid was taking place: "We knew they were looking for us."[23]

The US Navy Launches their Mission

In the Gulf of Tonkin, the next few hours were full of speculation and tension as the carriers launched their aircraft, timed to arrive over Hanoi as

Capable of flying over Mach 3 and at altitudes of 80,000ft, the SR-71 Blackbird carried out high-altitude reconnaissance missions over Son Tay. Having just come into service in 1966, the Blackbird was already playing an integral role in gathering intelligence over Southeast Asia. The photos of Son Tay were invaluable to planners and could be taken without tipping off the North Vietnamese. (USAF)

22 Gargus, 2022
23 Hall

the rescue was underway. Earlier, commanders had alerted those not privy to the approaching launches to prepare for action that night. On the USS *Wainwright*, the loudspeaker came alive as the XO interrupted the start of movie night, "Gentlemen, this is the Executive Officer. Tonight, the *Wainwright* will be engaged in operations anticipated to evoke a hostile response from North Vietnam. We will go to General Quarters at midnight. That is all."

The diversionary attacks with 56 aircraft, launched from Task Force 77 carriers, caught the North Vietnamese off guard. The plan all along was for the Navy to draw fire from Son Tay by staging simulated strikes against targets in the Haiphong Harbor area and North Vietnam. The size of the strike package impressed the ship crews. Fifty years later, Retired Rear Admiral Lawrence C. Chambers, then the Commander Air Boss of the *Oriskany* commented, "We knew it was big when we launched every flyable F-8, A-6s, and A-7s, plus the Willy Fudd. But we didn't know the mission until after recovery."[24]

Seven A-6 Intruders and 20 A-7 Corsairs would make runs on these targets, while CAP aircraft included 12 F-4s and F-8s. Six EC-1s and 14 anti-submarine warfare, tanker, and other support aircraft also filled the skies.

In the three tracks and three Iron Hand, anti-SAM, orbits, naval aviators fired off three Shrikes at active Fan Song radars in Haiphong and dropped a total of 190 flares. Slow to react to the first wave of naval aircraft, and untested since the March 31, 1968 halt in bombing north of the 20th parallel, the North Vietnamese were ready for the second wave coming over Haiphong Harbor and were quicker on the trigger. Runs over the harbor dispersed chaff confusing the enemy into thinking the Americans were mining the harbor.

The early warning detectors at Na San failed to report the Americans approaching Son Tay and air defense systems were unprepared. When they finally perked up, they unleashed their SA-2 SAMs in a blind barrage of desperation. Lieutenant "Bull" Durham, in his F-8 from the USS *Oriskany*, described the action as "nonstop SAM launches. Nobody was anywhere near the SAM sites, so the North Vietnamese launched them straight up in a barrage mode. Still, it was more hostile fire in two hours than I had seen in two cruises."[25] The US Navy diversionary aircraft had accomplished that part of the mission, diverting attention away from western approaches and out east toward the harbor. Caught

Eighteen A-7 Corsair IIs from the USS *Oriskany*, like these, flew missions north and south of Haiphong Harbor, dropping flares, and diverting North Vietnamese attention away from Son Tay. Nine A-7s from the USS *Ranger* flew "Iron Hand" anti-aircraft suppression and Rescue Combat Air Patrol (RESCAP) missions. (US Navy)

24 Gargus
25 Gargus, Pt 3

flat-footed or preferring to use SAMs, the North Vietnamese never launched their MIGs to challenge the overwhelming American air superiority.

Firebird 5 Goes Down

The F-105G Wild Weasels, armed only with two AGM-45 Shrike missiles, endured the most enemy fire. This would be the first time since 1968 US aircraft would be over Hanoi, and the SAM fire was as intense as expected. Captain Ted Lowry recalled a call for F-105G volunteers on November 19 and then the actual briefing on November 20. For the mission, about which they only knew it was in support of a ground operation, they were to remain over the objective until all friendlies had left the area – potentially, an awfully long time.

The F-105Gs faced 16 SAM launches and responded in kind firing eight Shrikes at the SAM sites. Although the crews were confident that they had hit the SAM sites, they were not 100 percent sure. The SAM operators knew not to lock on to targets headed their way and waited until aircraft began a turn. Unless the Americans had a plane lined up ready to fire behind the lead aircraft making a turn, the SAM operators could get off a shot.

An F-105G, Firebird 3, had two SAMs headed toward it. Within one mile of the SAM impact, the pilot dropped to below 5,000ft and as the SAMs pursued it, he pulled up. The first SAM missed and detonated harmlessly behind it. The second SAM exploded near the left wing, setting it on fire momentarily before the pilot managed to regain control and fly out of harm's way.

Meanwhile, another SAM rocked an F-105G, Firebird 5, with Pilot Major Kilgus and Captain Lowry, who had already avoided three SAMs. Firebird 5 lost its stability augmentation system and was leaking fuel from ruptured fuel tanks. Lowry asked Kilgus if they should leave and Kilgus responded, no, "the airplane is still flyable, and we have people down there. We need to stay." Thinking they could still refuel and get out safely, Kilgus called for a

THE AIR BATTLE OVER SON TAY

Simultaneous to the ground assault, a carefully choreographed air operation was underway that saw over 100 aircraft involved in the largest air operation over North Vietnam since the bombing halt of 1968. Navy aircraft from USS *Ranger* and *USS Oriskany*, like the A-7 Corsair IIs in the upper left, conducted diversionary raids or SAM suppression "Iron Hand" missions over Haiphong Harbor and Hanoi. C-130s *Cherry 1* and *Cherry 2*, center left, would lead the helicopters and A-1 Skyraiders to Son Tay and then drop flares and battlefield simulators around Son Tay to confuse the North Vietnamese where main attack was occurring. Air Force A-1 Skyraiders, bottom right, would fly close air support to drive back any North Vietnamese ground forces converging on Son Tay to stop the rescue. The North Vietnamese air defenses, once they realized what was happening, fought back ferociously, unleashing a steady barrage of SA-2 SAMs at the American aircraft, successfully hitting two. Firebird 3, a F-105 Thunderchief, was hit first and had to leave the battle space. Firebird 5, another F-105 Thunderchief took its place and was hit in turn. Pilot Major Donald W. Kilgus and Weapons Operator Captain Clarence T. Lowry were forced to eject at 0315hrs on November 21 and were rescued several hours later.

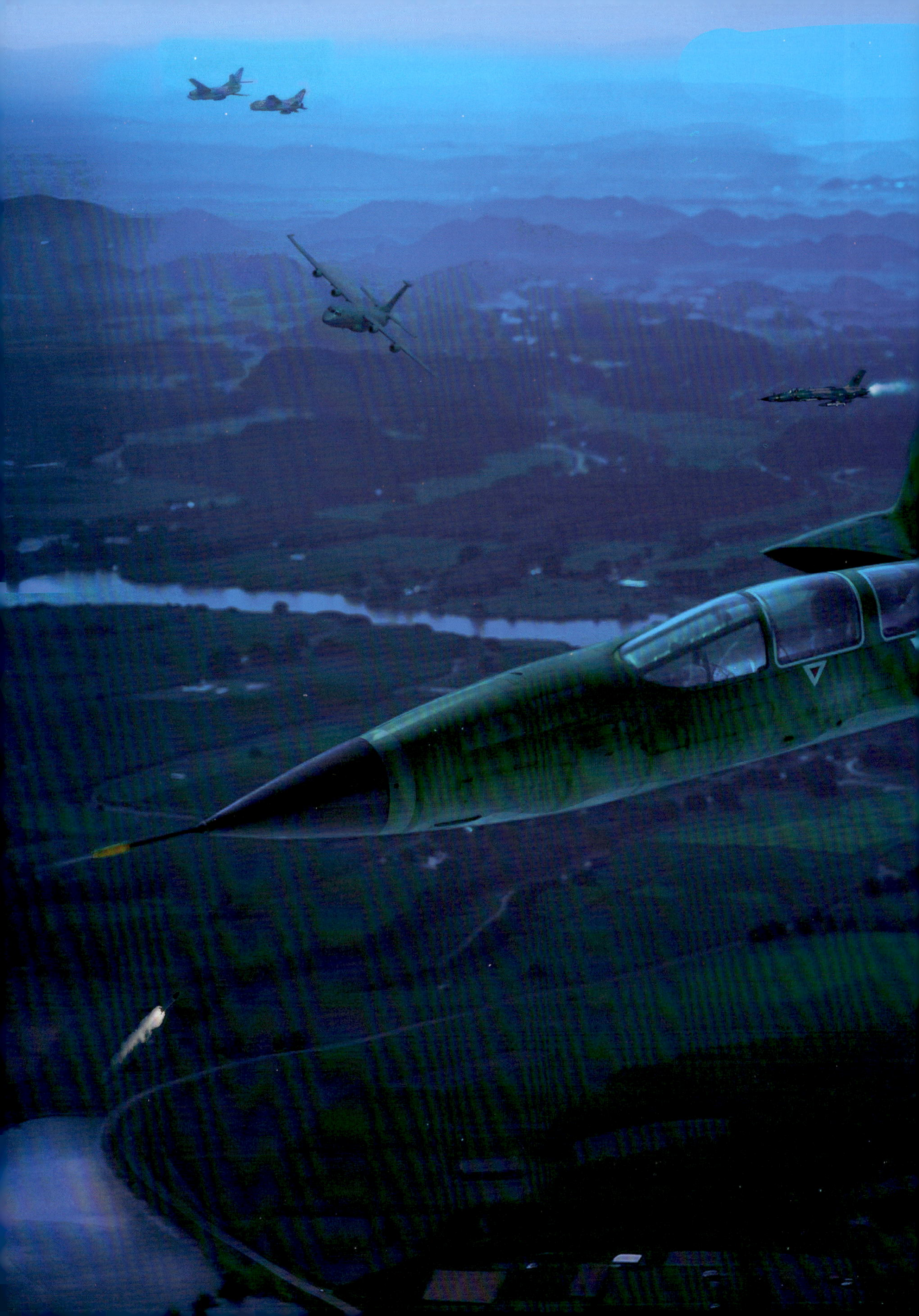

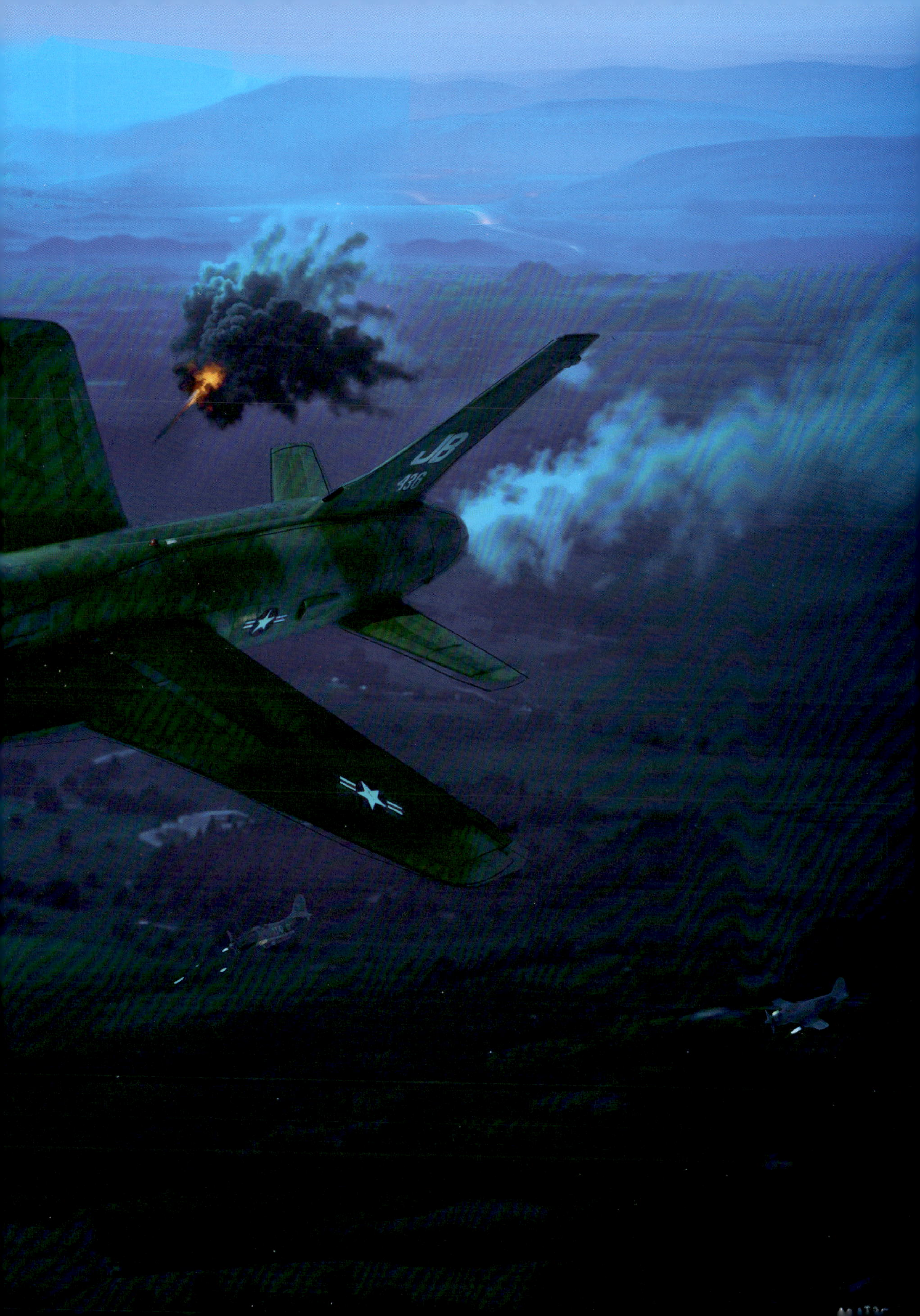
JB
436

The USS *Ranger* launched six F-4 Phantoms as a Combat Air Patrols (CAP) over the target area of the Navy diversionary raids. At one point, there were over 115 aircraft over the skies of North Vietnam conducting the raid, supporting the raid, or as a diversion. Despite the crowded airspace and flurry of anti-aircraft activity, only one plane was shot down, and all personnel returned safely. (US Navy)

tanker, but it was not going to arrive in time. Finally, Kilgus calmly said, "Ted we don't have enough gas to get home. Put the SAFE areas in the doppler and we'll head there." The crew headed toward Plaine des Jarres where the engines finally flamed out at 32,000ft. As the plane descended, the crew punched out at 12,000ft after Kilgus said, "Ted, it's time for you to go."[26] The F-4D MIG CAP aircraft orbited over the crew of the downed Firebird 5.

Extraction and Rescue

On the ground, disappointment in not finding POWs took a back seat now to getting the raiding party out safely. Only 14 minutes into the raid, Simons made a net call, based on the absence of the POWs, ordering the ground forces to "Prepare to withdraw to other LZ for extraction." The HH-53s took off from the holding areas and were back outside the camp. Britton's *Apple 1* took Meadows' team on board, plus the *Banana* crew, and then Sydnor's team. Remaining behind were the security group, the pathfinders, and the Marshalling Area Control Officer.

As *Apple 1* took off and headed west, *Apple 2* came in to pick up the remaining 33 men – Simons' team, part of Sydnor's, and Meadows'. Simons' LZ security fired their M79 40mm grenade launchers at four vehicles approaching. Meadows ran into the prison courtyard to blow up *Banana* still resting in the courtyard where it had deliberately "crashed" just 20 minutes earlier.

Twenty-seven minutes into the mission, *Apple 2* lifted off. On board, there was a moment of concern that they had left someone behind in the darkness and fast-moving operation. In the darkness, without cabin lights, several counts were made until the commanders were satisfied. A total of 59 men were on board, 25 on *Apple 1* and 34 on *Apple 2*.

They were not out of the woods yet. The helicopters headed west, staying as low as possible until they were able to ascend to over 1,500ft. The rear ramp gunner called out, "*Banana* just exploded!" as planned. They still

26 Buckler, 275–76

had to make it out of North Vietnam; with the NVA now fully on alert and determined to take down American aircraft, the raiding party still had to be wary. The helicopters took evasive maneuvers and dropped to minimum altitude as one of the A-1 Skyraiders unleashed its rockets into a ridge line just west of the Black River and F-105s were spotted in their vicinity.

Apple 3 remained on the ground the longest, waiting to see if anyone was left behind, then finally took off to join the others. But when Firebird 5, the F-105G hit by a SAM, was reported down in Plaine des Jarres, *Apple 5* moved to provide eyes on the downed crew. *Apple 2* linked up with 3 and headed home. After deciding the Fulton Recovery System would not work because of the terrain and the two crew being in separate locations, the rescue was turned over to *Apple 4* and *Apple 5*, which refueled via one of the HC-130 tankers and then headed to the search and rescue area.

Upon arrival, *Apple 4* and 5 spotted a C-130A dropping flares in two locations about a half mile apart, and the two helicopters took up positions in the south and north of the likely location of the crew. Judging the rescue to be too hazardous to complete at night, the aircraft withdrew. Lowry, admitting he was scared "witless" of being in enemy territory, settled down for some sleep. While *Apple 4* and 5 were refueling again, Number 5 was called back to the SAR area to pinpoint the crew and call in the SAR A-1 Skyraider. At dawn, *Apple 4* and 5 managed to pick up Lowry and Kilgus and headed back to Udorn.

By mid-morning of November 21, all aircraft and crew were safely back on the ground or on their ships. The mission was over. Described as the most densely packed night action for the US Navy in the conflict, not a single Navy aircraft was lost to enemy fire. General Manor would later write the actions of Carrier Task Force 77, "were vital to the overall success of the mission."

As rescue tactics evolved, A-1 Skyraiders working in tandem with HH-53 Jolly Green Giants became one of the indelible images of the war. While the helicopters picked up their charges, the Skyraiders flew Close Air Support (CAS) missions to keep back any enemy forces converging on the Americans. During the war, over 3,800 men were rescued, at the cost of 71 rescuers killed. (USAF)

THE AFTERMATH

Shock Among the Raiders and the Political Fallout Back Home

Back in Washington the Pentagon watch officer received the news and unceremoniously announced to the Command Authority office, "There are no prisoners in Son Tay!" Lieutenant General John Vogt, JCS Director of Operations, called Kissinger's Assistant General Haig to tell him, "Looks like a bust, Al. No prisoners." General Westmoreland and others were disgusted, complaining of the intelligence failure and the disaster. Vogt pointed out that the raiders had all made it back and a look at what did go wrong would be forthcoming.[27] At the White House, the shock of the empty camp was interspersed with the need to focus on Operation *Freedom Bait* strikes the next day. Kissinger wanted the Department of Defense to announce the Son Tay raid and the follow-on strike either the next day, "or as soon as Hanoi screams."

During the long flight back to Thailand, the men, exhausted and dumbfounded at finding no POWs, barely spoke. Manor met Simons at Udorn RTAFB to hear for himself the prisoners were gone. Disgusted, Simons said it was obvious the camp had been emptied for weeks, if not months. Even the shackles the raiders had spent so much time practicing cutting with their acetylene torches were gone. In Thailand when the men returned, in silent testament to the expected outcome were two C-141 medical transports waiting for the POWs that never came. The raiders were angry, silent, and ignored the "Welcome Home" banners, curious onlookers, food, and refreshments laid out in expectation of a successful mission. The men were soaked in sweat, battered from intense combat, disappointed in what had transpired, and could only sit down and pass around a bottle.

27 Schemmer, 220

Despite their exhaustion, waiting for them at the airfield were intelligence officers who wanted to debrief them on what had happened. Intelligence personnel greeted the pilots with "wide grins across their faces and seemed higher than kites" expecting to hear wonderful news of a rescue, only to turn pale white when the news sank in. Apparently, during the head counts of the raiders, some interpreted the radio calls as counting freed POWs.[28]

Manor and Simons were immediately summoned back to Washington. Before departing on the long flight back, Simons wanted to talk to the men. Less than 24 hours before, Simons had given them a rousing talk on the mission and the men had been excited to rescue their fellow Americans. Now, Simons spoke to the men, silently wondering what had gone wrong. He spoke of how proud he was,

> I know you are disappointed. We had the place right by the ass. But you have nothing to feel bad about, nothing to be ashamed of. You did your job, and you did it well as any combat commander could ask of you. We do not have a thing to be ashamed of. The operation, as far as what you did, was successful. You could not have done it better.[29]

On November 21, Manor sent Moorer and McCain a message stating, "the courage demonstrated by these truly outstanding individuals who participated in and over the objective area is admirable and I am personally convinced, beyond any doubt, that this force would have recovered all the POWs in that prison had they been there, as reported, upon assignment of the mission."[30] President Nixon was similarly informed of the heroics by Kissinger in a memo on November 21 outlining the events at Son Tay, concluding, "the task group carried out their mission in a highly professional manner and would have recovered any prisoners if they had been there."

Despite the empty camp, Manor and Simons learned President Nixon was proud of the mission, and he wanted to personally decorate the heroes brought back. Besides Manor and Simons, two enlisted men had to be decorated along with them. Simons objected saying all the men deserved recognition. Political considerations were driving the awards ceremony for a White House desperate to brag about something. If the awards ceremony was to be public, then more details of the raid would come out, contradicting previous planning and in sharp contrast to the months of secrecy leading up to the raid. Although there was some uneasiness in giving the briefing, the men haggled over the exact wording of how to sell the mission in a positive

President Nixon presents Sergeant First Class Tyrone Adderly the Distinguished Service Cross for his actions as part of Redwine Security Element 2. Armed with an M79 40mm grenade launcher, Adderly and his team's original objective of clearing an isolated pumphouse and securing the north end of the canal changed to clearing compound buildings when Plan Green went into effect. (Nixon Library)

28 Waresh
29 Schemmer, 222
30 Schemmer, 222

On December 9, 1970 Defence Secretary Melvin Laird visits Fort Bragg to present awards to the Son Tay raiders. In all, the Green Berets and Air Force personnel would receive Five Air Force Crosses, Seven Distinguished Service Awards, twenty-four Distinguished Flying Crosses, and eighty-eight Silver Stars. (US Army)

light, with Simons arguing that the mission should be spoken of proudly, "This is something that Americans traditionally do for Americans."[31]

That afternoon, Laird, Moorer, Manor, and Simons stepped before the Washington Press Corps. After discussing Hanoi's "adamant refusal" to exchange prisoners of war and the poor treatment of prisoners, some of whom were dying at the POW camps, Laird announced that after months of planning a rescue mission was launched. After several minutes, Laird finally said, "regrettably, the rescue team discovered that the camp had recently been vacated. No prisoners were found." The reporters asked many questions the men could not answer because the details were still classified, or they did not have the full reports from the mission yet. With limited information and in an already acrimonious relationship with the Nixon White House, critics painted the mission as a failure.

Nixon was accused of mounting the mission for political reasons and engaging in a new, and dangerous, according to Senator J. William Fulbright, Chairman of the Senate Foreign Relations Committee, "major escalation of the war." Others in the House and Senate vacillated between full support and outright criticism. Senator Henry Jackson said the attempt was warranted. Senator Edward M. Kennedy said he admired the courage of the men, but "I just deplore the policy that permitted them to go." Senator Birch Baya feared the raid might lead to Hanoi executing POWs and criticized the raid as the "John Wayne approach." Senator Robert Dole, introduced a resolution in honor of the raiders, "demonstrating American concern." Congressman Charles Vanick was incredulous that military intelligence had failed. Minority leader Gerald R. Ford hoped for further operations. Congressman Robert Legett said it sounded like "the scriptwriter of a grade C war movie" planned the mission.

The Senate Foreign Relations Committee called Laird to explain the raid. With the raid just a few days old, there was not much new Laird could say and he braced himself for criticism. Senator Fulbright did not doubt the men were brave but questioned whether "it was a wise attack." Laird said the mission, of which he admitted, there was "a fifty-fifty chance of returning with prisoners of war" was also about "letting the world know we cared." Laird, a former politician himself, pointedly told Fulbright, "I am very disappointed you have doubts about this."

Relations between the Pentagon and legislatures continued to sour as information came out contradicting Laird's testimony because Laird could not release the information, or the full report was not yet in. For example, Laird could not adequately address the intelligence errors and timing of messaging. In questions about the *Freeedom Bait* air strikes conducted just a few hours after the Son Tay mission, Laird had to untangle why those strikes were related to the shoot-down of reconnaissance aircraft and not

31 Schemmer, 226

the POW camp raid. Worse, when Laird talked about casualties, he only cited two – the sprained ankle and a gunshot wound – neglecting to mention the downed F-105. Laird was on the defense a few days later, when, despite Laird's assurances that he had worked with the CIA on the mission, Senator Fulbright said he had spoken to Richard Helms, Director of the CIA, who said the CIA was not consulted about the mission.

Fulbright took the failure to find the POWs personally. When Senator Dole introduced a resolution a few days after the raid to honor the rescue team, Fulbright blocked it on the grounds that passing the resolution might be seen as an endorsement of President Nixon's war efforts. On December 8, Fulbright again rejected the resolution (even though it passed in the House 347 to 15), stating that "officials knew there were no prisoners there and that the mission had other purposes."

Ignoring the hostility from some elected officials and anti-war activists, President Nixon personally decorated four of the Son Tay raiders on November 25 after an earlier private meeting with Moorer and Simons. Simons received the Distinguished Service Cross for "extraordinary heroism," and Army Sergeant First Class Tyrone J. Adderly also received the DSC for his actions that "eliminated the threat to the force." Air Force Technical Sergeant Leroy M. Wright, injured in the foot when *Banana* intentionally crashed inside Son Tay, received the Air Force Cross. Finally, General Leroy Manor received the Distinguished Service Medal. Nixon described the rescue attempt as "incomparable bravery and efficiency." He described that each man volunteered for the mission, knowing that there was a "50 percent chance that he might lose his life."

On November 26, the Hanoi government finally admitted the Americans had landed in North Vietnam, calling the mission futile, resulting in American casualties. Soviet propaganda newspaper *Pravda* claimed the raid was "spreading the land war into the territory of North Vietnam."

President Nixon greets a select group of the Son Tay raiders on November 25, 1970. Technical Sergeant Leroy M. Wright receives the Air Force Cross while still on crutches after being injured when *Banana* landed hard inside the Son Tay camp. Behind him is Sergeant Tyrone J. Adderly who received the Distinguished Service Cross for his part in assaulting several buildings. In the background, Colonel Arthur "Bull" Simons looks on, proud of his men. (Getty)

In a call between Haig and Nixon on November 28, Haig said the military viewed the mission as a "shot in the arm that they needed. To them it was a major breakthrough of national leadership with respect to the military." Haig said the men felt it was "the same as the Doolittle raids on Tokyo." Nixon signaled he was ready to try again, "it's up to them. If they come up with another plan, we'll go through with it. We've got a lot of bright people in the military. We're not sending them to War Colleges just to learn the history of the Napoleonic campaigns, are we?" Nixon concluded, "I say the greatest failure is not trying. If you try and don't succeed it's not a failure, it's just a lack of success in one instance. These boys did a hell of a job." Haig responded, "yes, and you're backing them up and immediately recognizing them had a tremendous impact on the military."

On Wednesday December 9, the Secretary of Defense arrived at Fort Bragg to personally decorate the raiders. The men earned four Distinguished Service Crosses and 50 Silver Stars. The Air Force recognized 43 Air Force participants with the Air Force Cross and Cataldo received a Silver Star, for his gallant and unselfish actions. But, as with everything else about the raid, the awards almost did not happen. The original plan was to present Simons with two Silver Stars, while 22 Bronze Stars with the "V" device for Valor would also be presented, and 30 would get a Commendation medal. Simons exploded at the insult, took his case to the Army Vice Chief of Staff, and threatened his men would turn down the awards. The Department of Defense relented and upgraded the medals. Murray, who had been wounded in the leg, received the only Purple Heart.

Not as widely known as the release of POWs in Hanoi, was the February 12, 1973 POW exchange at Loc Ninh, South Vietnam where twenty-eight Americans were exchanged for captured Viet Cong fighters. These Americans were held in South Vietnam, Laos, and Cambodia. Injured Captain David Baker sits in the hospital tent awaiting handover to the Americans. (USAF)

What Happened to the POWs?

As the Son Tay raiders were collecting their well-earned medals, a nagging question remained that would haunt the mission from then on – when were the POWs moved and why? More haunting was the fact that, at the last minute, intelligence had been picking up that the Son Tay prisoners were missing, but this was not acted upon or it was dismissed because things were in motion that could not be turned off. At the 1127th intelligence workshop, analysts finally read a letter from a POW on November 20, the day of the raid, that said they had been moved in early July.[32] Kissinger, part of Nixon's inner circle who had to approve the plan, confirmed this later stating he knew of the letter stating the camp was closed on July 14. The analysts thought this meant the gates were locked for security and the camp was still in use. In any case, Kissinger later said the information was considered insufficient to bring to the attention of the White House in the final briefings. But if the POWs had moved in

32 Veith, 266

July, why was there still photo evidence somebody was there? General Manor later reported that by vegetation growth that summer, it was evident the camp was unoccupied, but then later somebody cleared the vegetation, and started gardens, leading some analysts to conclude somebody was there. Circumstantial evidence of the camp showed it had held prisoners off and on over the years including latrines, litter, shutters, livestock, and ongoing repairs, as shown by the bags of cement found in one cell. It just was not in use when the raiders stormed it.

In exchange for twenty-eight American POWs held in enemy territory in South Vietnam and Cambodia, the Paris Peace Accords called for the release of Viet Cong and North Vietnamese. Here they wait to be turned over to the North Vietnamese on February 12, 1973 at Loc Ninh, South Vietnam. (USAF)

Manor's official report was just as puzzling. In the report, he noted a change in activity around Son Tay throughout the reconnaissance missions, but all for different reasons. SR-71 and drone missions showed increases in truck and vehicle activity south and west of the objective and spotted an Early Warning/Ground Intercept training site about 3⅓ miles southeast of the objective. The increase in vehicle traffic was attributed to driver training activity, construction, and harvesting. Then a report on October 3, showed a significant decrease in activity before increasing again between November 2 and November 6, but it was unclear if this was related to changes in anti-aircraft and troop movements around the camp. Later, the After-Action Report summarized that there was a definite decrease in activity around the compound between June 6 and October 3.

The CIA was introspective on what went wrong in a declassified secret 1984 study on intelligence efforts in Vietnam. The report verified that the POWs left the camp in July 1970, but put the responsibility of disseminating the evidence on the DIA because the Department of Defense owned the raid including the intelligence aspects. But the CIA was also vague in what it was detecting. The CIA on November 25, 1970, said its imagery analysts, having earlier confirmed Son Tay was a prison site, received its last photographs for analysis on November 21. In it the CIA confirmed the only change in the camp's appearance was the change in grass coverage. Earlier photographs had shown the open ground covered with grass, but in November it showed the same location sparsely covered in grass, indicating some type of activity. The Joint Chiefs of Staff understood the DIA could not guarantee the POWs would be there but pressed ahead with the raid. Shortly before the launch, the DIA informed Chairman Admiral Moorer and Secretary Laird that new evidence showed most, if not all, POWs had already been moved from Son Tay. A 1984 CIA review of intelligence operations in Vietnam showed this vital information never reached other members of the JCS or President Nixon.

November 23, 1970, President Nixon meets Colonel "Bull" Simons and General Leroy Manor. Defence Secretary Melvin Laird has inscribed the photo with "With best wishes and a job well done. Congratulations!" Henry Kissinger and Admiral Thomas Moorer look on. While the mood appears celebratory, the missing POWs hang over them. (Nixon Library)

Some speculated that the missing prisoners issue was related to an American effort to disrupt the weather over North Vietnam. Under Operation *Popeye* from March 1967 until July 1972, the CIA and Department of Defense flew over 2,600 cloud-seeding sorties over the North. Whether it worked or was just a coincidence, rainfall increased which slowed traffic down the Ho Chi Minh Trail. With over 270 sorties flown over an area near Son Tay, the waterways around Son Tay were overflowing, threatening the camp. A commander could have made the decision to move the prisoners because of the rain and floods. With *Popeye* a closely held secret and the Son Tay raid even more guarded, it was unlikely that commanders knew how *Popeye* would affect the mission. Former North Vietnamese officers were dismissive of the suggestion that flooding forced the Son Tay POW relocation because flooding in the area was predictable and even found the suggestion laughable.

One other odd reason for the missing POWs came out decades later showing the cultural misunderstandings that were a hallmark of the Vietnam War. The Son Tay POWs had been insistent that they hold separate Catholic and Protestant religious services, the North Vietnamese felt that moving them to a larger prison in Hanoi would make separating the prisoners by faith easier, which would bring praise from the international community. Dan Hoi prison, or as the POWs called it: "Camp Faith," received its final batch of Son Tay prisoners on July 14. With no POWs there, the Son Tay compound served other purposes, making it seem there was still POW activity there.

Another avenue of investigation was whether a leak had tipped off the North Vietnamese who then moved the POWs. Sully Fontaine, an American intelligence officer, was tasked to uncover a leak. After a fruitless investigation in the US and Southeast Asia, looking at all angles, he concluded there was no leak. On November 25, a North Vietnamese source with close contacts in Son Tay told a DIA officer that the prisoners were moved frequently and that there was no advanced knowledge of the raid. The copilot of *Apple 3*, years later, said he doubted there was any leak. If there had been, the NVA would have laid a trap for all the aircraft, loitering over Son Tay like sitting ducks.

Hanoi, always looking to exploit any engagement for propaganda value, remained quiet about the raid. The wreckage of *Banana* in the compound, the amount of gear left behind, and the absence of POWs could have given them a great propaganda coup. It would have been easy for the North Vietnamese to point to the raid as a failure of America, claimed they downed the helicopter, chased away the invaders, and proved all POWs were being held elsewhere in good conditions. Instead, Hanoi concentrated on responding to the near simultaneous US air raids of Operation *Freedom Bait* in response to North Vietnam firing upon US reconnaissance aircraft. A couple of days later, the Hanoi leadership talked about American air raids on Hanoi – the diversionary attacks by Task Force 77 – and mentioned American aircraft strafing a POW camp. Nearly a full week went by before Hanoi finally said there had been a POW rescue attempt that killed many civilians and wounded some POWs.

Colonel General Phung The Thai, NVA Deputy Chief of the General Staff during the raid, later wrote, "This may have been the most painful, most humiliating incident of my entire military career." The official North Vietnamese history said the raid showed a severe shortcoming of the air

After the raid, the North Vietnamese gathered the gear left behind by the Americans. The discarded gear and weapons, bore testimony to the ferocious raid and the audacity of the Americans to strike deep inside North Vietnam. Among the gear was a bullhorn used to announce to the POWs the raiders were American, anti-tank LAWs, ammunition, helmets, and the diversionary firefight simulators. (USAF)

defenses and, "the primary reason for this shortcoming was a low spirit of combat readiness and our failure to anticipate that the enemy would use helicopters supported by fighters to make such a deep penetration into our rear area to rescue their pilots."[33]

The Mystery of the Secondary School

One of the biggest mysteries of Operation *Kingpin* remains the identity of the enemy force at the Secondary School. There is no doubt that Colonel Simons and the 22 men of Greenleaf decimated an enemy unit when *Apple 1* inadvertently landed on top of a hornet's nest.

Post-raid after-action reporting said the enemy forces Greenleaf fought with were taller than North Vietnamese, "5 feet 10 inches to 6 feet, Oriental, not wearing normal NVA dress, but instead T-shirts and fitted dark undershorts" and they were "much better equipped" than the guards at Son Tay. The Americans "were unable to determine their nationality." Reporting indicated up to 200 of the mysterious enemy were killed. Nearly every published work since the raid mentions the mysterious force, but no documents have surfaced confirming exactly who they were.

It was no secret the Chinese and Russians were operating in North Vietnam, either supplying weapons and war materiel or training the NVA in their use. The Secondary School compound could have simply been the barracks for a Chinese detachment in the area for training and maintaining the many air defense systems in the area. Captain Udo Walther, commander of the Greenleaf group, said in an interview they definitely killed Chinese and he even took a Chinese belt buckle from a body, giving it to POW advocate, H. Ross Perot, years later.[34]

Despite it being an accidental engagement, nobody had any sympathy for those killed at the Secondary School. Chinese forces, known as "Headhunters," had been actively involved in tracking and killing American and allied Special Forces operating in Laos and North Vietnam. The CIA Special Assistant to Director Richard Helms, when asked if the unknown force consisted of Chinese, said that was "distinctly probable."[35] The other possibility, explaining the size of the enemy, but connected to the headhunters, is that they were hand-picked Soviet-trained men from the 305th Airborne Brigade, tasked to track down and kill the American MACV-SOG units.[36]

The undeclared war between China and the United States over the skies of North Vietnam was well known, but the ground war was more secretive because of the units involved and nobody, especially when the United States and China were feeling each other out for renewed relations, wanted to admit Americans and Chinese ground forces had fought it out in North Vietnam. Whether by intention or by accident, it is reasonably certain that the men assaulting the Secondary School decimated a Chinese force.

33 Gargus, Air Commando, 13
34 Walker
35 Marder
36 Plaster

ANALYSIS AND CONCLUSION

It is commonly believed that Hanoi concluded that if the Americans could strike anywhere, the POWs needed to be consolidated in more secure facilities. Many POW accounts speak of how the morale of all the POWs was boosted as word reached them of the attempted raid. Their treatment improved remarkably at the hands of their captors, and they knew America had not forgotten about them. Regardless of the controversy back home over the raid, every American combatant knew the decision was correct, especially in light of the torture and deaths of American POWs in the camps.

Treatment of the POWs actually began to improve following the death of Ho Chi Minh in September 1969 and the decision by the US to publicly attack the North Vietnamese over the treatment of the POWs. The movement of POWs to more consolidated locations had begun earlier. In the summer of 1970, a large group of prisoners were moved to Dan Hoi, Camp Faith, about 10 miles from Hanoi where the facilities were much better, with one former POW describing his treatment as "the best I had while in prison, and the closest we ever came to humane treatment under the Geneva Agreements."[37] Morale soared among the POWs as they came together in large numbers at the camps, as six camps, including Son Tay, closed before the raid. Interestingly, the improved morale was predicted by the CIA in a memo to General Blackburn on July 1, 1970, stating, "There is little question but that the occurrence of the operation itself, even if it achieves only very limited success, will have a major positive impact on the remaining prisoners." The raid even shook up the North Vietnamese guards. One former POW later told Captain Waldron, copilot of *Apple 3*, that the guards at their camp nearby were as "wide as silver dollars, afraid you might

37 Rochester, 18

Captured Viet Cong, in their POW uniforms wait to be turned over to the North Vietnamese on February 12, 1973 at Loc Ninh, South Vietnam. Some of the Viet Cong and North Vietnamese refused to return to North Vietnamese control, threatening to derail the exchange. (USAF)

come back."[38] One POW, however, felt differently. Major Kenneth Cordier, already in his fourth year of captivity, was crushed by news of the failure, "the raid convinced me that there was no hope we would ever get out of North Vietnam. They would only attempt a rescue mission if there was no other way."[39] On the home front, families of the POWs generally applauded the raid. Immediately after the raid, two camps closed. By 1970, negotiations with Hanoi partially hinged on the treatment of the POWs and Hanoi was willing to make amends to get the United States out of Southeast Asia. Their treatment and the conditions of the POW camps were still horrendous, but there was some improvement in the remaining three years before they were released.

Regardless, the raid was a staggering achievement. It showed that the United States was capable of pulling off a large-scale raid, deep behind enemy lines with little preparation time. Considering the raid concept had only originated in May 1970, it was an amazing accomplishment. The raid required the development of new tactics, marrying up a mixed batch of personnel into a cohesive fighting force, a logistical challenge of moving equipment and materials to training sites and onward in absolute security, and conducting an assault with incredible precision without a loss of a single raider. It was something few expected the United States, or any nation, could pull off. The carefully choreographed ballet of Air Force and Navy aircraft in the skies over North Vietnam, planned in absolute secrecy, only suffered one downed plane, Firebird 5, a F-105, was lost. The air portion is even more amazing considering within hours of the Son Tay raid, Operation *Freedom Bait* airstrikes hit North Vietnam, in response to the downing of an Air Force reconnaissance RF-4C on November 13. In the six hours before Typhoon Patsy forced the strikes to end, the Seventh Air Force and Seventh Fleet flew more than 200 sorties, striking SAMs, fuel dumps, supply convoys, and other targets of opportunity.

Unfortunately, the absence of POWs overshadows everything. Reconnaissance missions and intelligence analysis are always a difficult proposition, but in this case, the mission was given the highest priority and General Manor later remarked, "We practically had a blank check … it was the only time that somebody gave me a job and the resources with which to do it." Planners and commanders had SR-71s, drones, and even men on the ground to monitor the POWs. But after the initial discoveries, intelligence

38 Author interview
39 Dorr, 165

became less and less conclusive and the planners knew something was off. Nevertheless, momentum was carrying the raid forward and it seemed nobody wanted to take the responsibility of turning it off with so much riding on it. Lieutenant General Donald V. Bennett, Director of the DIA said 24 hours before the mission, "It looks like Son Tay is empty. The prisoners have been moved." General Blackburn, puzzled over the shaky intelligence, still decided to proceed with the mission. "Had

I known, I'd have called it off. But I didn't want to know the truth. I just wanted any shred of evidence to let us hang in there."[40] The mission had morphed into something bigger than the rescue of the POWs themselves. This mission was inextricably tied to political considerations of a White House under relentless criticism, a military reeling from failures in Vietnam, a chance to influence the Paris peace talks, and a demonstration of American power. Unfortunately, as the *Bright Light* missions had proven over the years, rescuing American POWs was always going to be near impossible.

This is where intelligence sharing came up short. With something this complicated, a streamlined system was needed for information to reach planners rapidly. Unfortunately, a number of factors kept that from fruition. First, the Cold War meant everyone was paranoid that the Soviets could find any bit of information and discover a clandestine mission. This fear meant the intelligence became so compartmentalized it became almost useless. The paranoia also altered the flights of the reconnaissance aircraft and even uninformed photo interpreters missed critical details. Good information was even delayed because the command and control of some of it rested as far away as Nebraska and not in theater. Even sharing weather reports was complicated by secrecy. By November 1970, all the information was there that the POWs were gone, but the right people did not have all the information. An especially damning CIA memo was sent on December 4 to Senator Helms that said the CIA had had all indications that the POWs had been moved and photos from November 6 clearly showed vegetation patterns indicating the POWs were gone. Nevertheless, General Blackburn responded, "the raid was then in train." The memo also indicated that Secretary Laird "acknowledged that he had seen the information but decided to proceed with the operation anyway."

Had the raid suffered casualties, and no POWs rescued, it would have been known as a catastrophic, demoralizing, embarrassing failure. Instead, the missing POWs are regarded as a fluke to an otherwise brilliant concept and execution.

On February 12, 1973, Brigadier General Stan McClellan has intense discussions over the final details of the prisoner exchange at Loc Ninh, South Vietnam. Though not as widely known as the Hanoi POW release, this was equally as important, bringing back Americans who were held in even worse conditions in North Vietnamese-controlled South Vietnam, Laos, and Cambodia. (USAF)

40 Haas, 328

EPILOGUE

On a bright April 27, 1973, a crowd gathered in San Francisco for a ticker-tape parade for the Son Tay raiders, sponsored by eccentric Texas millionaire H. Ross Perot for $250,000. The Electronic Data Systems founder had been heavily involved in the issue of prisoners of war in Vietnam and wanted to honor them. In a letter he sent to the raiders, he wrote that the former POWs "would like to meet you and personally thank you, as their first official act after returning home." Perched on the back of a red convertible, smoking a cigar, and wearing his Class A uniform was Colonel Arthur D. "Bull" Simons, obviously enjoying the moment, with the crowd recognizing his men for a mission that did not accomplish its objective. Yet, here they were basking in the limelight along with POWs released from North Vietnam as part of Operation *Homecoming* that saw the release of 591 POWs (as of 2024, 1,577 Americans are still listed as missing). At the Fremont Hotel, celebrities like John Wayne, Ernst Borgnine, and others congratulated them. It was a star-studded event, but what stood out in everyone's mind was the gratitude the POWs had for their would-be rescuers. Every one of them said the rescue attempt was a tremendous morale booster, had rattled the North, and ensured the POWs were treated better. Although it would be another two years before NVA tanks rolled into Saigon, the American war was essentially over, and Operation *Kingpin* had already earned its legendary status in the annals of commando raids.

BIBLIOGRAPHY

Most of the information about Operation *Kingpin* was declassified shortly after the raid. These documents contain every imaginable detail of the planning and execution, from seemingly mundane information on budgets to gripping after-action narratives by personnel. These documents can be found on various websites such as:

https://www.esd.whs.mil/Portals/54/Documents/FOID/Reading%20Room/Personnel_Related/97-F-1230_DOC_01-Son_Tay_Raid.pdf

https://documents.theblackvault.com/documents/dod/readingroom/16/974.pdf

Department of Defense MIA files: a huge trove of documents from the DOD, including everything from the Son Tay Raid, intelligence reports, post-war recovery efforts, and post-war MIA/POW sightings can be found here: https://downloads.paperlessarchives.com/p/dztgwt/

An audio recording of the raid transmissions can be found on the "Military Tales" YouTube channel: https://www.youtube.com/watch?v=ozMhCf4Zjk8

Avriett, Carole Engle, *Under the Cover of Light: The Extraordinary Story of USAF Col Thomas Curtis's 7½-year Captivity in North Vietnam*, Tyndale House Publishers, Carol Stream, IL, 2017.

Berger, Carl, ed., *The United States Air Force in Southeast Asia, 1961–1973*. Office of Air Force History, 1984.

Brokhausen, Nick, *We Few: US Special Forces in Vietnam*. Casemate Publishers, 2018.

Buckler, Terry, *Who Will Go: Into the Son Tay POW Camp*. Palmetto Publishing, Charleston, NC, 2020.

Cawthorne, Nigel, *Warrior Elite*. Berkeley, CA, Ulysses Press, 2012.

Chinnery, Philip D., *Air Commando*. Naval Institute Press, Annapolis, MD, 1994.

CIA, August 1967 Memo, https://www.cia.gov/readingroom/docs/DOC_0000013869.pdf

CIA, February 1970 Memo, https://www.cia.gov/readingroom/docs/DOC_0001437706.pdf

CIA, May 1970 Memo, https://www.cia.gov/readingroom/docs/DOC_0001437707.pdf

CIA, July 1970 Memo, https://www.cia.gov/readingroom/docs/CIA-RDP80R01720R000600070022-1.pdf

CIA, November 1979 Memo, https://www.cia.gov/readingroom/docs/DOC_0001437709.pdf

Cleaver, Thomas McKelvey, *The Tonkin Gulf Yacht Club*. Osprey, Oxford, UK, 2021.

Commander JCS Joint Contingency Task Group Report on The Son Tay Prisoner of War Rescue Operations Part One, https://mcoecbamcoepwprd01.blob.core.usgovcloudapi.net/library/Documents/Hardcopy/paper/Son%20Tay%20Prisoner%20of%20War%20Rescue%20Operation%20Part%20I.pdf

Cox, Samuel J., *US Navy in Vietnam: Late 1970 to December 1971*, Naval History and Heritage Command, H-Gram 059-2, 2021, https://www.history.navy.mil/about-us/leadership/director/directors-corner/h-grams/h-gram-059/h-059-2.html

Dallek, Robert, *Nixon and Kissinger: Partners in Power*. Harper Collins, New York, 2007.

Department of State, Office of the Historian, *Foreign Relations of the US, 1969–1976*, Volume VII, Vietnam, July 1970–January 1972, Documents 56, 66, 71, 73 https://history.state.gov/

Dorr, Robert F. and Bishop, Chris, *Vietnam Air War Debrief*. Aerospace Publishing Ltd, London, 1996.

Evans, Andy and Llinares, Rick, *US Air Force Special Operations Command*. Sam Publications, Bedford, UK, 2010.

Gargus, Colonel John G., "Recollections of the Son Tay Raiders," *Air Commando Journal*, Vol. 9, Issue 2, October 2020.

Gargus, Colonel John G., *The Greatest Naval Deception of the Vietnam War*, US Naval Institute, *Naval History Magazine* Parts 1, 2, 3, 2022.

Gargus, John, *The Son Tay Raid: American POWs in Vietnam Were Not Forgotten*. Texas A&M Press, College Station, TX, 2010.

Gillespie, Robert M., *Black Ops Vietnam*. Naval Institute Press, Annapolis, MD, 2011.

Guenon, Jr., William A., Captain, *Secret and Dangerous: Night of the Son Tay POW Raid*. East Lowell, MA, King Printing Company, Inc., 2002.

Guidry, Colonel Ronald D. (ret.), "Intelligence Gathering by Drones," *Air Commando Journal*, Vol. 3, Issue 1, Winter/Spring 2014.

Haas, Colonel Michael E., *Apollo's Warriors: United States Air Force Special Operations during the Cold War*. Air University Press, Alabama, 1997.

Hall, Cheryl, *Dallas Morning News*, July 13, 2019.

Harker, David, "Army Veteran Recalls his Time as POW During Vietnam," September 18, 2020, https://news.va.gov/79008/army-veteran-recalls-time-pow-vietnam/

Hoe, Alan, *The Quiet Professional*, The University Press of Kentucky, Lexington, KY, 2011.

Hung, Dang Voung, *The Truth About Son Tay*, translated by Merle L. Pribbenow, Hanoi, 1978.

Isby, David C., *Leave No Man Behind: Liberation and Capture Missions*. Orion Books, London, UK, 2004.

JPRC Fact Sheet, https://www.loc.gov/item/powmia/pwmaster_114864/

Kamps, Charles T., *The History of the Vietnam War*. Aerospace Publishing Ltd, London, 1988.

Kissinger, Henry, *Ending the Vietnam War: A History of America's Involvement in and Extrication from the Vietnam War*. Simon & Schuster, New York, NY, 2003.

Library of Congress, Son Tay Files, https://www.loc.gov/item/powmia/pwmaster_114973/

Mersky, Peter B. and Polmar, Norman, *The Naval Air War in Vietnam*. Nautical & Aviation Publishing, Annapolis, MD, 1981.

Naval History and Heritage Command, "Chapter 3: The Years of Combat 1965–1968," https://www.history.navy.mil/research/library/online-reading-room/title-list-alphabetically/b/by-sea-air-land-marolda/chapter-3-the-years-of-combat-1965-1968.html

New York Times, December 9, 1970.

Nixon, Richard, *The Memoirs of Richard Nixon*. Grosset & Dunlap, New York, NY, 1978.

Operation *Kingpin* Operations Order, https://www.esd.whs.mil/Portals/54/Documents/FOID/Reading%20Room/Personnel_Related/97-F-1230_DOC_12-Son_Tay_Raid.pdf

Palmer, Bruce, General, "US Intelligence in Vietnam," CIA, 1984, https://www.cia.gov/static/ff6447a7cfcf258d277bee21807d2828/Palmer-USIntelligenceandVietnam-web.pdf

Petersen, Michael B., The Vietnam Cauldron: Defense Intelligence in the War in Southeast Asia. DIA Historical Research Branch, 2012.

Plaster, John L., *SOG: The Secret Wars of America's Commandos in Vietnam*. New American Library, New York, NY, 1997.

Risner, Robinson, *The Passing of the Night: My Seven Years as a Prisoner of the North Vietnamese*. Konecky & Konecky, 2004.

Schemmer, Benjamin F., *The Raid*. Harper & Row, New York, NY, 1976.

Shultz, Jr., Richard H., *The Secret War Against Hanoi: The Untold Story of Spies, Saboteurs, and Covert Warriors in North Vietnam*. Harper Perennial, 2000.

Stanton, Shelby L., *Green Berets at War*. Presidio Press, Novato, CA, 1985.

Thigpen, Jerry L., *The Praetorian Starship*. Air University Press, Alabama, 2001.

Thompson, Wayne, *To Hanoi and Back: The USAF and North Vietnam, 1966–1973*, Air Forces History and Museums Program, Washington, DC, 2000.

Tilford, Jr., Earl H., *Search and Rescue in Southeast Asia, 1961–1975*. Office of USAF History, 1980.

Townley, Alvin, *Captured: An American Prisoner of War in North Vietnam*. Scholastic Focus, 2019.

Townley, Alvin, *Defiant: The POWs Who Endured Vietnam's Most Infamous Prison*. St. Martin's Griffin, 2015.

Turner, Spencer, ed., *Encyclopedia of the Vietnam War*. Oxford University Press, Oxford, UK, 2000.

Veith, George J., *Code Name Bright Light: The Untold Story of US POW Rescue Efforts During the Vietnam War*.The Free Press, New York, NY, 1998.

Waldron, Lieutenant Colonel Thomas R. (ret.), *I Flew with Heroes: A True Story of Rescue and Recovery During the Vietnam War Including the Raid at Son Tay*. Create Space Publishing, Charleston, SC, 2012.

Walker, Gret, *At the Hurricane's Eye: US Special Forces Operations from Vietnam to Desert Storm*. New York, NY, Ivy Books, 1994.

Walker, Greg, "The Real Son Tay Raid," Special Forces Association, Chapter LXXVIII, February, 2022, https://www.specialforces78.com/the-real-son-tay-raid-51-years-later/

Waresh, John, "A-1 Participation in the Son Tay Raid," November 21, 1970, https://web.archive.org/web/20080704175227/http://www.jollygreen.org/Stories/john_waresh.htm

Whitcomb, Darrel D., *On a Steel Horse I Ride: A History of the MH-53 Pave Low Helicopters in War and Peace*. Air University Press, Alabama, 2012.

INDEX

References to image are in **bold**.